I0268176

PEACHES

Copyright © C. Thornton 2013

The right of C. Thornton to be identified as author of this work has been asserted in accordance with the Copyright, Designs and Patents Act, 1988.

All rights reserved. No part of this book may be reproduced or transmitted by any person or entity (including Google, Amazon or similar organisations) in any form or by any means, electronic or mechanical, including photocopying, recording or by any information storage and retrieval system, without prior permission in writing from the publisher.

National Library of Australia Cataloguing-in-Publication entry

Author: Thornton, C., author.

Title: Peaches / C. Thornton.

ISBN: 9781925110487 (paperback)

Series: Rare and heritage fruit ; Set 1, no. 8.

Notes: Includes bibliographical references and index.

Subjects: Peach.
Peach--Varieties.

Dewey Number: 641.3

ABN 67 099 575 078

PO Box 9113, Brighton, 3186, Victoria, Australia
www.leavesofgoldpress.com

RARE AND HERITAGE FRUIT
CULTIVARS #8

PEACHES

C. Thornton

- RARE AND HERITAGE FRUIT -
THE SERIES

SET #1

RARE AND HERITAGE FRUIT
- CULTIVARS -

1 Apples
2 Cider Apples
3 Crabapples
4 European Pears
5 Nashi Pears
6 Perry Pears
7 Apricots
8 Peaches
9 Nectarines
10 European Plums
11 Japanese Plums
12 Cherries
13 Figs
14 Cactus & Dragon Fruits
15 Oranges
16 Lemons
17 Limes
18 Mandarins & Grapefruit
19 Kumquats, Calamondins & Chinottos
20 Rare & Unusual Citrus
21 Nuts
22 Berries & Small Fruits
23 Quinces
24 Guavas & Feijoas
25 Table Grapes
26 Wine Grapes
27 Avocados
28 Rare & Unusual Fruits
  and more...

SET #2

RARE AND HERITAGE FRUIT
- GROWING -

1 Propagating Fruit Plants (other than grafting)
2 Grafting and Budding Fruit Trees
3 Planting Fruit Trees and Shrubs
4 Care of Fruit Trees (compost, mulch, water etc)
5 Pruning Fruit Trees and Shrubs
6 Training and Espaliering Fruit Trees and Shrubs
7 Harvesting and Storage of Fruit
8 Pests and Diseases of Fruit Trees and Shrubs

SET #3

RARE AND HERITAGE FRUIT
- PRESERVING -

1 Fruit Preserving (drying, crystallizing, bottling etc.)
2 Cider Making
3 Perry Making ('pear cider')
4 Fruit Wine Making
5 Fruit Spirits and Liqueurs Making
6 Fruit Schnapps Making

www.leavesofgoldpress.com

With thanks to
Richard Hawkey, peach enthusiast
and orchardist extraordinaire,
for sharing the Bathurst list.

ABOUT RARE AND HERITAGE FRUIT[1]

This book is one of a series written for 'backyard farmers' of the 21st century. The series focuses on rare and heritage fruit in Australia, although it includes much information of interest to fruit enthusiasts in every country.

For the purpose of this series, rare fruits are species neither indigenous to nor commercially cultivated in any given region.

'Heritage' or 'heirloom' fruits such as old-fashioned varieties[2] of apple, quince, fig, plum, peach and pear are increasingly popular due to their diverse flavours, excellent nutritional qualities and other desirable characteristics.

It is much easier for modern supermarkets to offer only a limited range of fruit cultivars (i.e. varieties) to consumers, instead of dozens of different kinds of apples, pears etc. During the 19th and early 20th centuries, however, the diversity was huge. Old nursery catalogues were filled with numerous named

---

1   Note: this introduction is identical in every handbook in the Rare and Heritage Fruit series.

2   The correct term in this case is 'cultivars'; however most people are more familiar with the term 'varieties' and although it is not strictly accurate, we use the terms interchangeably in this series.

varieties of fruits, nuts and berries, few of which are available these days.

What are heritage fruits? 'An heirloom plant, heirloom variety, heritage fruit (Australia), or (especially in the UK) heirloom vegetable is an old cultivar that is "still maintained by gardeners and farmers particularly in isolated or ethnic communities".[3]

'These may have been commonly grown during earlier periods in human history, but are not used in modern large-scale agriculture. Many heirloom vegetables have kept their traits through open pollination, while fruit varieties such as apples have been propagated over the centuries through grafts and cuttings.'[4]

Broadly speaking, heritage fruits are historic cultivars; those which have initially been selected or bred by human beings and given officially recognised names, before being propagated by successive generations of growers, retaining their genetic integrity far beyond the normal life-span of an individual plant; those which are not protected by a private plant-breeders' licence, but instead belong to the public at large. They are the legacy of our ancestors; living heirlooms; part of humanity's horticultural, vintage and culinary heritage.

Fruit enthusiasts around the globe are currently reviving our horticultural legacy by renovating old orchards and identifying rare, historic fruit varieties. The goal is to make a much wider range of fruit trees available again to the home gardener.

This series of handbooks aims to help.

---

3   Whealy, K. (1990). "Seed Savers Exchange: preserving our genetic heritage".(*Transactions of the Illinois State Horticultural Society 123: 80–84.*)
4   *'Heirloom plants'* Wikipedia. Accessed 2013

STORIES

Like people, every fruit cultivar has a name and a story. Take the Granny Smith apple, for example - the most successful Australian apple, instantly identifiable with its smooth green skin, exported world-wide, and now cultivated in numerous countries.

This famous cultivar began in the 1860s as a tiny seedling that chanced to spring up in a compost heap. An orchardist by the name of Mrs Maria Ann Smith lived with her ailing husband in Eastwood, New South Wales (now a suburb of Sydney). She was in her late sixties, a hard worker and the mother of many children.

One autumn day, as usual, Maria Smith drove her horse-drawn wagon home from the Sydney markets, where she had been selling the fruit from her orchard. The wagon possibly contained a few wooden crates she had purchased after selling her produce, in which to transport the next load of wares. One or two leftover Tasmanian-grown French Crab apples might still have been lying in the crates, somewhat battered and past their prime. Imagine 'Granny' Smith, her grey hair tucked up inside her bonnet, trudging down to the creek from which the household drew its water and dumping their decaying remains on its banks.

There in that damp spot, sinking into compost-rich soil, the apple pips lay throughout the winter months. Come spring, one of them split open and a tiny white rootlet appeared. It swiftly bored downwards, stood up and threw off its black seed-case, revealing two perfect, green cotyledons.

The leaves quickly multiplied as the seedling grew, Maria spied it next time she walked down to the creek, the hems of her long black skirts rustling through the ferns. She nurtured the infant tree until it grew up and bore fruit. When at last she picked the first green-skinned apple and took a bite, she must have been surprised by the crisp, hard flesh and sharp taste. No doubt she used it to make pies and other desserts for her sick husband and numerous grand-children, thus discovering that this new cultivar was good for both cooking and eating.

She shared the apples with friends and neighbours, allowing them to cut scion-wood from her tree and graft their own cloned versions. Locally, word of the apple's qualities spread.

'Smith died only a couple years after her discovery, but dozens of Granny Smith apple trees lived on in her neighbours' orchards. Her new cultivar did not receive widespread attention until, in 1890, it was exhibited as 'Smith's Seedling' at the Castle Hill Agricultural and Horticultural Show. The following year it won the prize for cooking apples under the name 'Granny Smith's Seedling'.

'The apple became a hit. In 1895 the New South Wales Department of Agriculture officially recognized the cultivar and began growing it at the Government Experimental Station in Bathurst, New South Wales, recommending its properties as a late-picking cooking apple for potential export.

'During the first half of the 20th century the government actively promoted the apple, leading to its widespread acceptance. However, its worldwide fame grew from the fact that it was such a good 'keeper'. Because of its excellent shelf life the Granny Smith could be transported over long distances in cold storage and in most seasons. Granny Smiths were exported in enormous quantities after the First World War, and by 1975 forty percent of Australia's apple crop was Granny Smiths. By this time the apple was being grown extensively elsewhere in the southern hemisphere, as well as in France, Great Britain and the United States.'

'The advent of the Granny Smith Apple is now celebrated annually in Eastwood with the Granny Smith Festival.[5]

Fruit cultivar stories continue to arise in the 21st century. From AAP, February 21, 2010, 'Mudgee Farmer Bruce Davis Creates New Fruit':

'Is it a plum? Is it a peach? It's probably a pleach as it's a morph of the two tasty stone fruits. Whatever it is, it's a love child of the two, accidentally created by a retired NSW farmer.

'Bruce Davis from Mudgee in the state's central west couldn't believe it when he discovered he had grown a cross between a peach and a plum. The fruit looks like a peach from the outside, but resembles a red plum when bitten into. 'The unusual fruit is believed to be the first of its kind ever grown in the state.

'Mr Davis grows peach and blood plum trees alongside each other and believes the peach/plum tree may have grown from compost that contained plum seeds.

'"It's a really interesting piece of fruit and it's very tasty," Mr Davis said.

'A cross between a plum and an apricot, known as a pluot, has been grown in the past, but a peach and a plum is a new combination for NSW, Primary Industries Minister Steve Whan said.

'Industry and Investment NSW Mudgee horticulturist Susan Marte said this was the first time she had heard of anyone accidentally crossing the two fruits.'

---

5   *'Granny Smith' Wikipedia. Accessed 2013*

NAMES

The origin of the Mudgee pleach and the Granny Smith apple are two of many intriguing fruit stories, but sometimes the name - or names - of cultivars tells yet another story, an etymological one. Names may be inspired by the place a new cultivar was discovered, by the person who selected or bred it, by the shape, flavour, colour or use of the fruit, by an event that took place around the time of discovery, by somebody's sweetheart, or any number of other factors.

Names, too, may be multiplied.

The Granny Smith apple was discovered after the advent of newspapers. If you forgot what the prize-winning cultivar was called, you could look it up and there it would be, in black and white. This was not the case for many ancient cultivars.

The Granny Smith apple's probable mother, the French Crab, itself boasts twenty-six listed synonyms, probably invented by forgetful apple-growers.

Another instance of numerous synonyms is the French cider apple whose name is Calville Rouge D'Hiver, meaning 'Calville Winter Red'. It arose in the late 1500s, and as its popularity spread across Europe, the first thing that happened was that people translated the name into their own language: 'Teli Piros Kalvil', 'Roter Winter Calville, 'Calvilla Rossa di Pasqua', 'Cerveny Zimni Hranac' etc.

Next, when absent-minded peasants could not remember the name of this excellent red fruit, they gave it another one. Imagine a weather-beaten farmer in some isolated French village scratching his beard and musing, 'It was something to do with "Calville". 'Calville Rouge,' perchance?' Across the valley in another village, a cider-brewer was knitting his (or her) puzzled brow and saying, 'It was something to do with winter, I am thinking, or was it autumn? "Pomme d'Automne"?' Further afield, a third Frenchman shrugged his shoulders and declared, 'Devil take me if I can remember how it is called, but it is big and red like the heart of a bull, so let us name it '"Coeur de Boeuf.'"

Fanciful, perhaps, but this might explain why, on the database of the UK's National Fruit Collection, there are more than a hundred synonyms listed for Calville Rouge D'Hiver.

Words are forever evolving. Even when cultivar names stay the same, the language around them is changing and their original meaning becomes lost in the mists of time.

One example of this is the grape cultivar Cabernet Sauvignon, which is considered a relatively new variety, being the product of a chance 17th century crossing between Cabernet franc and Sauvignon blanc.

'Cabernet franc' can be etymologically traced back to 'French Black Grape' (from the Latin word 'caput' which means 'black vine'). The word 'Sauvignon' is believed to be derived from the French 'sauvage', meaning 'wild' and to refer to the grape being a wild grapevine native to France. 'Blanc,' of course, means 'white'. 'Cabernet Sauvignon' no longer means 'Wild Black Grape' in modern French - that would translate as something like 'Vigne Noir Sauvage'. The ancient cultivar name has now taken on its own meaning and is virtually synonymous with the wine made from it.

It is interesting to compare typical cider apple names with, say, typical peach or perry pear names. French words abound among heritage cider apple cultivars, reflecting their roots in medieval Normandy. To the ears of English-speakers these names may sound rather mysterious and aristocratic, until you translate them: for example, Gros Bois, Jaune de Vitré, Moulin à Vent du Calvados, Noël des Champs, Belle Fille de la Manche, Petite Sorte du Parc Dufour and Groin D'âne translate respectively as Big Wood, Yellow Glass, Windmill of Calvados, Christmas Field, Beautiful Girl of the English Channel, Small Kind of Park of the Oven and Donkey's Groin.

Some names of heritage perry pears give us an insight into the bawdy, rustic humour of the perry-drinking English peasants who originally selected them; Ram's Cods, Startle Cock and Bloody Bastard to mention a few.

Heritage grape cultivars have names that come from all over Europe, particularly France and Italy.

Figs go back even further. Humans were cultivating them around 9400 BC, a thousand years before wheat and rye were domesticated. Their names, in English at least, are often drawn from their colour and their place of origin - Brown Turkey, White Adriatic, Black Genoa, Pink Jerusalem, Green Ischia ...

Peaches, a more 'modern' fruit in terms of their popularity and breeding, often bear invented names with fancy spellings, such as Florda Glo, Earligrande, Harbrite and Dixigem.

'IMMORTAL' DNA

Another major difference between stone fruit and fruits such as grapes, figs and apples is their ability to grow 'true' to their parents from seed. Stone fruits are far more homozygous than their ancient cousins the pomes (apples, pears etc.) and the grapes. Growers do graft them, but if you plant their seeds the new tree will bear fruit that's fairly similar to that of the parent tree. This means that the centuries-old grafting traditions, the fierce cherishing, the careful bequeathing and the meticulous labelling that accompany pome fruits, grapes and other heterozygotes are not seen as often in the world of peaches and nectarines. This is why many of their cultivar names seem so different, arising as they do from highly organised commercial breeding programmes of the 20th and 21st centuries.

Unlike the seedlings of say, peaches and nectarines, seedling apples are an example of 'extreme heterozygotes', in that rather than inheriting DNA from their parents to create a new apple with those characteristics, they are instead significantly different from their parents.'[6] (Humans are rather like apples in that way, though not as extreme.)

Returning to our green-skinned Australian apple - 'Because the Granny Smith is a chance (and rare) mutation, its seeds tend to produce trees whose fruit have a much less appealing taste. To preserve the exact genetic code of any plant variety, a stick of the wood has to be 'cloned'. It has to be grafted onto new roots (or planted directly into the ground, but this is uncommon for trees). Thus, all the Granny Smith apple trees grown today are cuttings of cuttings of cuttings from the original Smith tree in Sydney.'[7]

Cloning by grafting means that the heritage trees - and shrubs - which have survived through the years

---

6   *John Lloyd and John Mitchinson (2006). QI: The Complete First Series – QI Factoids*
7   *Stirzaker, Richard (2010). Out of the Scientist's Garden: A Story of Water and Food. Collingwood, VIC: CSIRO Pub.*

are genetically identical to their ancestors. Indeed, the heritage plants of today possess exactly the same genetic code as the original trees that arose centuries ago in Asia and Europe. For example, another heritage apple cultivar, 'Court Pendu Plat', is thought to be 1500 years old - the oldest one in existence. Introduced into Europe during Roman times, the living wood from that same tree flourishes to this day, right here in the Great Southern Land.

RARE AND HERITAGE FRUIT IN AUSTRALIA

Many of the rare and heritage fruits that exist in Australia today are clonally descended from plants brought to our shores by the early European settlers, when few, if any, quarantine laws existed. Good luck rather than good stock monitoring limited the number of plant diseases unintentionally imported during the early days of colonization. Fortunately, by 1879 it was recognised that in order to prevent the introduction of serious pests and diseases, quarantine measures were needed. In 1908, the Commonwealth Quarantine service came into operation and took over local quarantine stations in every Australian state.

However, before 1879, there was no limit to the varieties of fruiting plants that could be imported into this country. Many of those old genetic lines survive to this day but sadly, many others have been lost.

Fortunately, Australia is one of only two countries free of fire blight, a serious and ineradicable disease that wiped out millions of apple, pear, loquat and quince trees in Europe and the USA during the 1900s. This means that when certain heritage cultivars went extinct elsewhere, they remained safe in this country.

Some have now been restored to their region of origin, now grafted onto fire blight-resistant rootstock.

Over the course of the decades since 1879 Australian fruit growers imported (through quarantine) the latest new cultivars bred by overseas agricultural research stations. Year by year, as scientific advances in breeding and genetics were made, the older cultivars fell out of fashion and were swept aside in favour of the new. They, too, became part of our almost forgotten fruit inheritance.

COMMERCIAL CULTIVARS

Naturally, plant breeders strive to provide the products demanded by the market. Commercial orchardists want to purchase heavy-bearing trees with high disease resistance, whose fruit ripens all at the same time to save on picking costs. Wholesalers want fruit that keeps in storage for a long time without spoiling, and can be shipped without damage. Only firm-fleshed, bruise-resistant fruit will survive modern-day processing. After harvesting, apples, for instance, are tipped into crates, then passed along a conveyor belt through machinery that washes and brushes them clean of insecticides and dirt. This process removes some of the fruit's natural protective coating, so the machines re-apply a commercial grade wax before polishing them to a high shine and pasting a plastic label onto each one. Then the apples are packed into cartons for shipping to markets and stores.

Supermarket shoppers demand visually attractive fruit - large, regular in shape, unblemished and with highly coloured skin. Consumers also choose fruit with extra sugar content and juiciness.

All these characteristics, nonetheless, do not necessarily give rise to the best flavour or nutrition. To pick a tree-ripened fruit from your own back yard and bite into it is to experience the taste of fresh food as our forefathers knew it. Growing and preserving their own food, unconcerned with transportability and long storage times, they aimed for a wide variety of fruits, each of which had a unique and delicious taste.

Rare fruit, heritage and heirloom fruit enthusiasts across the world are reviving our horticultural legacy by renovating old orchards and sourcing 'lost' historic and unusual fruit varieties. Their goal is to encourage community participation and to make a wide range of fruit trees available again to the home gardener.

This series of handbooks aims to help.

WHY PRESERVE RARE AND HERITAGE FRUITS?

• They provide access to a wider range of unique and delicious flavours.
• We can enjoy the nutritional benefits of fresh, tree-ripened food.
• Biodiversity: The preservation of a wide range of vital genetic material helps to insure against the ravages of pests and diseases in the future.
• They allow a longer harvesting season, with early and late ripening.
• Culture: heritage varieties, with their interesting assortment of names, are living history.

Collections of heritage fruit trees are precious. Anyone who is the custodian of an old tree should treasure it.

CONTENTS

About Rare & Heritage Fruit ix

About Peaches xxiii

Peaches A - D 1

Peaches E - G 25

The Florida Peaches 26

Peaches H - K 59

The Harrow Peaches 60

The Haven Peaches 62

Peaches L - O 77

Peaches P - Z 89

Index 135

About Peaches

There are probably more than 4,000 peach and nectarine cultivars in the world, and new cultivars are continually being introduced from fruit tree breeding programs. This handbook contains a catalogue of heritage peach cultivars currently found in Australia. Most of the names are sourced from a list provided by the Bathurst Primary Industries Centre in New South Wales. Others come from various Australian plant nurseries and the Rare Fruit Society of South Australia.

The Bathurst Primary Industries Centre research plantings include stone fruit cultivar arboreta with a large number of heritage fruit trees, also known as 'Public Varieties' (as opposed to varieties privately licenced under Plant Breeders Rights; see below.)

From Bathurst's website: 'The current variety collections at the Centre are the result of many years of trialling public varieties. These tests provided detailed information to stone fruit growers until the 1990s. Limited access to private varieties resulted in the termination of the program. The varieties have continued to be available to industry and research institutes.

'The collections of peach, nectarine, plum and apricot varieties are still being maintained at the Centre. The collections are in the process of being rationalised to retain only the most important varieties...'

What this means is that Bathurst is no longer growing and maintaining every single one of the old stone fruit cultivars. Many on this list are now untraceable in this country, though they may well exist in orchards maintained by private individuals. As for public orchards—around a dozen old peach cultivars from Bathurst are growing at Werribee Park Heritage Orchard in Victoria, which is cared for by volunteers.

It is not easy to find information on some of the more obscure cultivars; nonetheless even those with unobtainable data have been listed here. The only ones not included are those which Bathurst labelled with a number only, such as '46A4' or '1-8'.

PEACHES: THEIR BACKGROUND

Of all the deciduous tree fruit varieties, the peach is ranked third in global economic importance after the apple and the pear.

Peaches are relative newcomers among the favourite fruits of the world. Peaches today look very different from the rather small, greenish-skinned, furry fruits they were originally. Over the centuries, selection and breeding by gardeners and horticulturists have led to the large, colourful, low-fuzz fruits of the 21st century.

In Europe, peach orchards existed from the late 19th century, but it was not until the middle of the 20th century, with advances in fruit breeding techniques, that the popularity of this fruit really exploded.

Wikipedia informs us: 'The peach, Prunus persica, is a deciduous tree, native to northwest China, where it was first domesticated and cultivated. The species name 'persica' refers to its widespread cultivation in Persia, whence it was transplanted to Europe. It belongs to the genus Prunus—which includes the cherry and plum—in the family Rosaceae (which includes strawberries and roses!). The peach is classified with the almond in the subgenus Amygdalus, distinguished from the other subgenera by the corrugated seed shell.

'It is thought that peaches were traded first to Asia and then to the Mediterranean and Europe, around two thousand years ago. The breeding of new peach cultivars now occurs mostly in the USA and Italy.'

THE PEACH INDUSTRY IN AUSTRALIA

Being suited to temperate regions, peaches are commercially grown in Australia's cooler southern states. The Murray-Goulburn Valley in Victoria produces 80% of canned peaches in this country, but there are also peach orchards in the Murrumbidgee in New South Wales and the Riverland area of South Australia. 'Golden Queen' is the cultivar usually processed for canning by the industry, but earlier and later-ripening cultivars prolong the canning season.

NECTARINES

Nectarines are really just smooth-skinned peaches, despite the fact that they are regarded commercially as different fruits. They originated as mutations of Prunus persica, and are known as 'Prunus persica variety nectarina'. Nectarines are smooth-skinned, while peaches have a light 'pubescence', i.e. a fuzzy skin.

CHILL REQUIREMENTS

Peach trees need cold weather during the winter in order for the buds to develop properly, so that the trees will bloom and come into leaf normally. 'The chilling requirement of a fruit-bearing tree is the minimum period of cold weather after which it will blossom. It is often expressed in chill hours, which can be calculated in different ways, all of which essentially involve adding up the total amount of time in a winter spent at certain temperatures. Apples have the highest chilling requirements of all fruit trees, followed by apricots and, lastly, peaches.' (*Wikipedia, 9th March 2015*)

Peach cultivars in Texas for example, range in their requirements from 100 chilling units (the FlordaGrande cultivar, zoned for low chill regions) to 1,000 units (Surecrop, zoned for high chill regions). Planting a low-chilling cultivar in a high-chill region risks loss of a year's harvest when an early bloom is hit by a spring frost. A high-chilling cultivar planted in a low-chill region will, quite likely, never fruit at all.

In America, for many decades, fruit breeders have been selecting 'low chill' cultivars to suit the climate of the southern states, where winters are too warm for the older cultivars. Australian fruit tree importers have been interested in these. Many of the peaches on Bathurst's list are low chill cultivars that originate from U.S. breeding programs.

Low chill cultivars include Maygold, Junegold, and Suwanee. Desertgold and Flordasun require even less chilling, and are sometimes called 'sub-tropical'. Junegold, Sunnyside, and Fairway cultivars are freestones adapted to warmer areas. Desertgold can be grown where winters are short. Other low chill peaches include Springold, Springcrest, Royal May, Flavourcrest, Redtop, Suncrest, Fayette, Summerset, and Fairtime.

BREEDING NEW PEACH CULTIVARS

As mentioned earlier, peaches are an extremely popular fruit. For hundreds of years there has been intense interest in peach breeding. These days, a successful new peach cultivar can bring enormous profit to whoever owns the licence. 'Plant breeders' rights (PBR), also known as plant variety rights (PVR), are rights granted to the breeder of a new variety of plant that give the breeder exclusive control over the propagating material (including seed, cuttings, divisions, tissue culture) and harvested material (cut flowers, fruit, foliage) of a new variety for a number of years.' (Wikipedia)

For example, the Angel Peach™ is protected by PBR at the time this book is published, meaning that it is illegal to propagate plant material from this cultivar under the 1994 PBR Act. Without these licences, plant breeders would have less incentive to spend time and money pursuing cultivars with highly prized characteristics.

Many of the older plant licences, however, have expired and the cultivars are freely available for propagation. Zee Lady and Earlicot are two examples.

'[Commercial] Peach breeding has favored cultivars with more firmness, more red colour, and shorter fuzz on fruit surface. These characteristics ease shipping and supermarket sales by improving eye appeal. However, this selection process has not necessarily led to increased flavour.'[1]

---

1   *'Peach' Wikipedia. Accessed 2013.*

DIFFERENCES BETWEEN PEACH CULTIVARS

FLESH COLOUR

Peaches are either yellow fleshed, white fleshed or red fleshed. Studies have shown that in general the western palate prefers yellow fleshed peaches while Japanese and Chinese consumers prefer white flesh. Because white peaches have lower acid levels and higher sugar levels, they also have a slightly sweeter taste. White peaches ripen faster, are more fragile and bruise more easily; thus they are harder to transport.

Red-fleshed peaches are rare in many countries, though they are popular in France (where they are called 'pêche de vigne') and New Zealand (where they usually go by the name of 'Blackboy Peach'). The USA has the clingstone peach 'Indian Blood', also known as 'Cherokee'. In Australia some private growers do raise 'blood peaches', whose flesh is lightly blotched with red. Other than those, the closest approximation to a red-fleshed peach available from Australian nurseries is the pleach, which is not a true peach but a cross between peach and a blood plum.

THE 'PIT' OR 'STONE'

Peaches and nectarines are either clingstone, freestone or semi clingstone.

Clingstone—The flesh adheres to the pit when the fruit is cut in half. Most early-season peach and nectarine cultivars are clingstones. Clingstone cultivars tend to have firm flesh.

Freestone—Cultivars with flesh that separates easily from the pit. Most cultivars used for fresh eating are freestone.

Semiclingstone or semifreestone—Fruit whose flesh separates easily from the stone when the peach is fully ripe.

Uses

Most peaches are classifed as 'dessert' fruit because they are delicious eaten fresh no matter what type of pit they have; however some are better for culinary purposes. The semi-free and freestone are the best peaches for making pies, freezing, drying and canning etc. because the flesh of these peaches is easier to separate from the pit. The semi-freestone and clingstone can be used for all purposes, but they require a little more work than the freestone fruits. Many people prefer to use the clingstone cultivars for jams, preserves, jellies, and pickles, as their flesh is firmer.

During a normal season, clingstone peaches ripen first, followed by semi-free, and freestone peaches in the order they are listed. Keep in mind that each season depends on the weather, and if there is a warm spring, peaches usually ripen earlier. After a cool spring, they generally ripen later.

Flesh Texture

Peaches are classified by flesh texture as either melting, nonmelting or hard.

Melting flesh peaches become softer as they ripen and will 'melt in your mouth' when they are fully mature. Most consumers prefer this type for fresh eating out of hand.

Nonmelting flesh peaches remain firm in texture when fully mature and never become melting.

Nonmelting flesh peaches typify most peaches that are used for commercial canning because they need to keep their shape. Some 'freestone, melting' types are canned but they represent a very small proportion of canned peaches.

The hard flesh type is very firm, even crispy when fully ripe. This type never melts and is typical of some white fleshed peaches from Asia.

(Source: Clemson Cooperative Extension)

Ripening times

Ripening times are important. Peaches have a short shelf-life, so a number of cultivars ripening sequentially are needed to maintain a supply of fruit during the summer months. If you choose to grow an early, a mid-season and a late cultivar in your home garden, you can supply yourself with fresh peaches for several months. Staggered ripening times also help to avoid a harvest glut such as occurs when all the fruit ripens at the same time.

Ripening times given in this book are a general guide only. Weather, altitude and other variables can cause annual variations, so that harvest dates of any given cultivar can vary. Very warm weather usually shortens the season and may cause cultivars to ripen at the same time. Early blossoming, combined with cool summer temperatures, may spread harvest dates over a longer period.

Blossom types

Most commercial cultivars have 'showy' blossoms, which are flowers with large pink petals. 'Nonshowy' blossoms have smaller, redder petals. Both are spectacularly beautiful.

POLLINATION

Most peach cultivars are self-fruitful although there are some self-unfruitful cultivars such as J.H. Hale and Candoka. These require the nearby presence of a different peach cultivar that blossoms around the same time.

OTHER DIFFERENCES

Peach cultivars can also differ in fruit size, tree vigour, pubescence and disease resistance.

BEAUTY AND FLAVOUR COMBINED

Peach trees are beautiful, especially in spring when they are covered with pink blossom. Some dwarf cultivars bred specifically to have ornamental value and bear great-tasting fruit include 'Snow Ballet, 'Rose Chiffon' and 'Bonanza'.

HOW TO TELL IF A PEACH IS RIPE

'Don't rely on colour alone to check for ripeness. Fully ripened peaches will have a delicious fragrance. Select fruits that give a little when you hold them firmly in your hand. If the peach is green around the stem, it's not ripe. Also, the skin should be completely filled out and the crease should be deep. If the skin is wrinkled, the peach is past its prime.

'If you're picking your own peaches from an orchard, pick those that separate easily from the tree. If it doesn't want to let go, it isn't ripe. Also, pull the fruits with equal pressure on both sides. Don't dig your fingertips into the flesh – you'll cause bruising. Don't pile your peaches deeply into buckets either, or those on the bottom will be bruised from the weight of their companions on top. Peaches should be stacked only 30-35 cm (12-14 inches) deep.'

(Source: A Guide to Peaches—HubPages)

HOW TO STORE PEACHES

'If you discover that the peaches you bought aren't quite ripe enough, leave them at room temperature for a couple of days to ripen. You can hasten this process by wrapping each peach in newspaper. This traps the ethylene gas emitted by the fruits, which will help ripen the flesh. Ripening occurs more rapidly in freestone fruit than in cling peaches. Note that if the peaches were very hard and green when picked, they'll get softer, but not riper.

'Once your peaches are soft, store them in your refrigerator crisper for up to five days.

'To keep peaches longer, freeze them. They must be frozen in liquid to avoid freezer burn and to maintain taste. The liquid is up to you. You can use apple juice, white grape juice, peach juice, pear juice, or a sugar syrup.

'To make the syrup, heat six cups of water with sugar until completely dissolved. For a light syrup, use two cups of sugar. For a medium syrup, use three cups of sugar, and for a sweet syrup, use four cups of sugar. Once the sugar has dissolved, let the syrup cool.

'To peel your peaches, just drop the washed fruit in boiling water for 30-45 seconds, depending on the size of the peaches. Remove them from their bath with a pierced spoon and place them in an ice-water bath for 3-5 minutes. The skins will slip off easily!

'Slice the peaches and place them in a bowl. Sprinkle the slices with lemon juice to prevent browning. Stir gently.

'Next, place the desired amount of peaches into freezer boxes or bags and cover with syrup solution. Remove any air from the bags and freeze. The peaches will keep for about 10 months in the freezer.'
(Source: A Guide to Peaches—HubPages)

STANDOUT PEACHES

During the collation of this catalogue, several peaches seemed to stand out from the rest. It can be said, of course, that the best peach is 'the one that's ripe at the time', but for flavour and appearance, vigour, hardiness and abundance, there are some that apparently excel all round. These include Anzac, Blackburn, Candoka, Candor, Clayton, Cresthaven, Dixigem, Dixired, Elberta, Ellerbe, Fay Elberta, Fragar, Golden Queen, J.H. Hale, Loring, O'Henry, Redhaven, Tatura 204, Tatura 211, Tropic Beauty, Tropic Snow and Zeelady.

DEFINITIONS

Culinary: culinary peaches are good for canning, bottling, drying, stewing, cooking and preserving.

Dessert: a dessert peach is one that is delicious eaten fresh, out of hand.

Nonbrowning flesh: flesh that shows relatively little discolouration when thawed after being frozen.

Pubescence: the fuzzy hairs on the fruit surface. They may be longish, short, thick or thin.

Self-fertile: a tree is self-fertile when it is able to produce fruit by fertilisation with its own pollen Self-fertile trees do not need another tree nearby to pollinate them. Most peaches are self-fertile.

'Splitstone' or 'split pit' in peaches can be caused by anything that makes the fruit bigger, such as too much fruit thinning, excess watering and fertilizing near harvest time, partial crop loss due to late frosts or heavy rains during the fruits' growth period.

Rare and Heritage Peach Cultivars

in Australia

A to D

Prunus Persica

NOTE: ALL RIPENING DATES ARE CALCULATED FOR THE SOUTHERN HEMISPHERE.

Abiacuto

This cultivar is recorded as held by the Rare Fruit Society of South Australia. No other information is available.

Afterglow

Ripens mid February—early March. No other information is available.

Albatros

Synonyms: Albatross
Provenance: South Africa, 1973
Use: Dessert, culinary
Flesh: Colour white, texture; melting
Stone: Cling
Fruit description: Diameter approximately 61 mm, shape; round with prominent suture, skin colour; green with a red blush. Moderate eating quality.
Blossom time: August
Ripening times Early to mid December
Pollination: Self-fruitful
Chilling requirements: Medium-low (201 - 400 hours)
Other information: Storage ability is moderate (around three weeks). The tree is highly productive.

Anzac

Synonyms: None known.
Provenance: Australia, circa 1900.
Use: Dessert, culinary. Best eaten fresh.
Flesh: Colour white.
Stone: Freestone

Fruit description: Large, round. Skin dark ruby red and cream. Exceptionally sweet taste, very good flavour.
Blossom time: Unknown
Ripening times: Not verified. Some say late December to early January, others say January to February.
Pollination: Self-fertile
Chilling requirements: Normal chill
Other information: The tree produces abundant fruit for about a month. Does not appear to be to susceptible to curly leaf.

Anzac Peaches. Photo: Garden Express

Baby Gold 5

Blossom time: Early September—early October
Ripening times: Mid January—late January

Baby Gold 6

Blossom time: Early September—early October
Ripening times: Mid February—late February

Beale

This cultivar is recorded as held by the Rare Fruit Society of South Australia. No other information is available.

Bendigo Beauty

Synonyms: None known
Provenance: Australia
Use: Dessert, culinary
Flesh: White and juicy.
Stone: Unknown
Fruit description: Excellent flavour but bruises easily. Skin colour red and cream.
Blossom time: Unknown
Ripening times: Early January
Pollination: Self-fertile
Chilling requirements: Unknown
Other information: Very good producer. Fruit gradually ripens over a number of weeks, not coming all at once.

Blackburn

Synonyms: Blackburn Elberta
Provenance: Unknown
Use: Dessert or culinary. Used for fresh fruit, stewing or drying.
Flesh: Yellow; firm; sweet; good texture.
Stone: Freestone
Fruit description: Larger and earlier than Elberta, flavour excellent. The skin has a deep pink blush

over a cream-green background. The fruit is juicy, with a very good flavour.
Blossom time: Unknown
Ripening times: Mid February (late season).
Pollination: Self-fertile. This peach is the pollinator for J.H.Hale's Million Dollar Peach – which is about the only peach that really needs a pollinator.
Chilling requirements: Unknown
Other information: A vigorous tree which is a heavy bearer.

Blackburn Elberta

see 'Blackburn'

Blackman

Blossom time: Early September—early October
Ripening times: Mid January

Blake

Flesh colour: Yellow
Stone: Freestone
Fruit description: Unknown
Blossom time: Mid September—early October
Ripening times: Early February—mid February
Chilling requirements: 750 hours
Other information: Bacterial spot susceptible

Boon County Seedling

Synonym: Boon Country Seedling
Provenance: Boone County is located in the U.S. state of West Virginia.
Use: A small-fruited root-stock cultivar.

BOYCE-ELBERTA

Synonyms: Boyce x Elberta
Provenance: A hybrid of 'Elberta' and 'Boyce'.
Use: Dessert, culinary
Flesh colour: Possibly yellow like 'Elberta'
Stone: Possibly freestone like 'Elberta'
Blossom time: Early September—early October
Ripening times: Mid February

BRIGGS RED MAY

Provenance: An old heritage cultivar
Use: Dessert and bottling.
Flesh colour: White.
Stone: Freestone
Fruit description: A medium to large round peach with a white skin and a bright red cheek. Sweet and juicy, with rich, delicious flavour. Melting flesh. One of the best early peach varieties.
Blossom time: Early September—early October
Ripening times: Late December
Pollination: Self-fertile.

Briggs Red May. Photo: Mount Alexander Fruit Gardens

Brighton

Synonyms: None known
Provenance: New York State 1972
Use: Dessert, culinary
Flesh colour: Yellow
Stone: Unknown
Fruit description: The fruit are medium in size, attractive red-skinned and of good quality, with a clingy flesh, sweet and juicy.
Blossom time: Early/mid September—early October
Ripening times: Mid December—early January
Pollination: Self-fertile
Chilling requirements: 750 hours
Other information: Brighton is an early-season variety that does well in cold areas. Moderately vigorous.

Candoka

Synonyms: None known
Provenance: Bred by American W.F. Ramsey and colleagues including Andy Gossman, a pharmacist from Minnesota USA. In 1932 Gossman patented Candoka, a 'fuzzless' peach. Assigned plant patent number 51, it was probably one of the first peaches to be patented. Its name was derived from 'Okanogan County.'
Use: Dessert, culinary
Flesh colour: Unknown. Flesh is firm.
Stone: Unknown
Fruit description: Very large and heavy, skin smooth and velvety, bright red-golden. Delicious, sweet flavour.
Blossom time: Mid September—early October

Ripening times: Early February—mid February
Pollination: Needs cross-pollination. Pollinated by most other peaches.
Chilling requirements: Unknown
Other information: Keeps well but bruises easily. Branches may have to be propped up while fruit is ripening, because it is so heavy.

An article from 'The Brewster Herald,' Brewster, Okanogan County, Washington, Septemberember 15, 1933 states:
'Brewster Candoka Peach Co. is New Local Organization To Set Out Large Orchard of New Variety.
The Brewster Candoka Peach Co. Inc. was organized last Wednesday in Brewster.
W.F. Ramsey, well known Okanogan Florist and principal originator of the new, popular peach, and D.S. Gamble are the organizers of the new company. They have several others who have planned on joining the peach growing company.
The newly organized company will plant 30 acres in Candoka peaches this year and increase their acreage until the company will have at least 100 acres within tree or four years.
The 'Candoka' is fast becoming the most popular peach on the market. it has a much higher colour, much firmer flesh, better keeping qualities and has a skin that is smooth as velvet. It does not drop as readily as its competitive brothers.

And from 'Charlie and the Giant Peach... and the Wayward Cherries: A History of Oliver Ranch. (Now known as Brock Farm) Oliver Ranch History As I Remember it in 1943'. Morrie Thomas, June 20, 2010:

> 'I believe that there was 110 acres of fruit trees planted on the property, including: cherries, peaches, apricots and pears. At one time it was even said to be the largest soft fruit orchard in the British Empire.
> 'The orchards came into full bearing in the early '40s. Along with the orchard, Charlie had also built a packing house. All the able-bodied males of the day were in the armed forces, so the available workforce was composed of local women and children. Between the orchard and the packing house, there would have been approximately 80 people working on the ranch in 1943.
> 'One of the varieties of peaches which came into production at that time was the Candoka peach—a peach with two serious drawbacks. Candoka was so large and heavy, the weight of them broke down the trees, plus they bruised easily, and thus were difficult to ship to market. To solve the shipping problem, all available teenagers were hired to work in the packing house folding large egg carton-type cardboard containers. As big as these containers were, each carton could only hold four of these huge peaches. My sister Dolly, cousin Ginny and I moved up to the ranch into one of the many picker cabins and were part of this early orchard experiment, which did not

prove successful, and the Candoka peach disappeared.'

Fortunately Candoka only disappeared from commercial use. This wonderful peach passed into the public domain and became a heritage fruit cultivar.

Candoka Peach, 1934. Artist: Royal Charles Steadman, b. 1875

CANDOR

Synonyms: None known

Provenance: Candor is a hybrid resulting from a cross of Redhaven with Erly-Red-Fre. It was released in 1965 and became the most widely grown and popular cultivar released from the North Carolina breeding program in the USA. It was grown extensively in many [warmer] southeastern states.

Use: Dessert, culinary

Flesh colour: Bright yellow, exhibiting slight red pigmentation at the pit.

Stone: Semi-freestone.
Fruit description: Fruit is medium in size. The shape is round-oblong with a slight point at the tip of the fruit. Pubescence (the peach-fuzz) is very light and short. Skin colour is an 80% mottled dark red blush over an attractive bright yellow ground colour. The flesh is firm and the texture is slightly coarse. Flesh flavour is excellent, but it is slightly more acidic than most peach cultivars. The flesh is not free until the fruit is soft-ripe. Split pits have been a problem in some years. Fruit are extremely resistant to flesh browning
Blossom time: Early September—early October
Ripening times: Mid December—late December
Pollination: Self-fertile
Chilling requirements: 950 hours
Other information: Trees of Candor are vigorous and bloom at the same time as Redhaven. Flower buds possess superior cold hardiness, and are very resistant to cold weather at bloom. Leaves and fruit are highly resistant to bacterial spot. Candor consistently produces heavy crops of fruit, even in years of adverse weather conditions. It is one of the most reliable early season cultivars.
The town of Candor, North Carolina, is known as the 'Home of the North Carolina Peach' and hosts the annual North Carolina Peach Festival.
Candor's popularity, however, was not to last forever. In August 2007 the Ontario Ministry of Agriculture and Food announced that Candor was one of the fresh market peach cultivars that had been have been dropped because they were 'no longer considered important.'

CARDINAL

Provenance: Unknown
Use: Dessert, culinary
Flesh colour: Yellow
Stone: Unknown
Fruit description: Medium size with yellow skin.
Blossom time: Early September—early October
Ripening times: Late December—early January
Pollination: Self-fertile
Chilling requirements: 950 hours
Other information: A small-growing, round-headed, ornamental flowering peach with dark-red double blossoms. A real showpiece in the spring.

CARMAN

Synonyms: Carmen
Provenance: A heritage peach passed down from one generation of peach farmer to another. A favorite white peach in the USA a century ago.
Use: Dessert, culinary
Flesh colour: White.
Stone: Unknown
Fruit description: Pale yellow skin with red blush on sunny side; rich, sweet and good flavour spiced by a hint of tartness. Oblate fruits are rich with syrupy juice tempered by subtle acidity. Luscious flesh that melts in the mouth.
Blossom time: Early September—early October
Ripening times: Mid January—late January
Pollination: Self-fertile
Chilling requirements: 700 hours.
Other information: The tree is vigorous and productive

Champion

Provenance: Unknown
Use: Dessert, culinary
Flesh colour: White
Stone: Freestone
Fruit description: Very large size, beautiful colour, good flavour; very hardy and valuable early peach. A red skinned, large, juicy dessert peach.
Blossom time: Unknown
Ripening times: Unknown
Pollination: Self-fertile
Chilling requirements: Unknown
Other information: None available

Prunus persica 'Champion'

China Flat

Provenance: A heritage cultivar first grown in China during the 19th century. The Chinese call them Peento, Peen To, or Pan tao. They are known elsewhere as paraguayos, saturn peaches, UFO peaches, flat peaches or 'doughnut'/'donut' peaches.

The peento peach, like all peaches, is native to China but it has only been cultivated in the west since circa 1869

Use: Dessert, culinary

Flesh colour: White. Texture: firm but melting.

Stone: Freestone. There is little to no fuzz on the skin.

Fruit description: Flat in shape, pale in colour and with a fragrant, delicate flavour. Very sweet, with not much acid. (See photo on page 90.)

Blossom time: Unknown

Ripening times: Unknown

Pollination: Self-fertile

Chilling requirements: 150 hours (low chill)

CLAYTON

Provenance: A cultivar from North Carolina, USA., Clayton resulted from a cross of Pekin x Candor. Released in 1976, this cultivar was named in honor of Dr. Carlyle N. Clayton.

Use: Dessert and culinary

Flesh colour: Deep yellow with red around the pit cavity. The flesh has good firmness and is melting with a fine texture. It is also highly resistant to flesh browning.

Stone: Freestone.

Fruit description: Fruit are excellent in flavour and very resistant to split pits. Clayton fruit are medium size, and fruit shape is round to slightly oblong, with a slight tip. Pubescence (peach skin fuzz) is very light and short. Clayton fruit have a beautiful bright red skin colour, covering about 75% of the fruit surface. The ground colour is a very attractive bright yellow. Clayton is one of

the most externally attractive peach cultivars available.
Blossom time: Mid September—early October
Ripening times: Early January—mid January
Pollination: Self-fertile
Chilling requirements: 950 hours
Other information: Trees of Clayton are vigorous and produce an extremely high number of flower buds. Very heavy fruit set is common. Therefore, in years of heavy fruit set, early and heavy fruit thinning is necessary to attain a good fruit size. Heavy flower bud production is an advantage in years of flower bud damage due to freezing temperatures, since a greater flower bud reserve exists to produce a potential fruit crop. Clayton is highly resistant to bacterial spot and also appears to possess resistance to peach leaf curl (*Taphrina deformans*).

Collins

Blossom time: Early September—early October
Ripening times: Mid December—early January

Colonel

Blossom time: Mid September—early October
Ripening times: Late December—mid January

Comanche

Synonyms: Commanche
Provenance: USA
Use: Dessert, culinary
Flesh colour: Yellow
Stone: Unknown

Fruit description: Unknown
Blossom time: Early September—early October
Ripening times: Mid January—late January
Pollination: Self-fertile
Chilling requirements: Unknown
Other information: Quite resistant to peach bacterial spot

Cornish

No information is available for this Bathurst cultivar.

Corona

This cultivar is recorded as held by the Rare Fruit Society of South Australia. No other information is available.

Coronet

Synonyms: None known
Provenance: Unknown
Use: Coronet is ideally used for fresh fruit, canning, stewing, baking and jam.
Flesh colour: Yellow
Stone: Freestone
Fruit description: A medium to large fruit with quite a sweet flavour.
Blossom time: Early September—early October
Ripening times: Early January—mid January
Pollination: Self-fertile
Chilling requirements: 700 hours
Other information: The tree is quite a heavy cropper and grows to approximately 4m x 4m.

Corowa

A rootstock, probably named for the town of Corowa iin the Australian state of New South Wales

Correll

Synonyms: None known.
Provenance: Correll resulted from a cross of Pekin x Candor, and was released in 1975. This cultivar was named in recognition of the late Professor Franklin E. Correll.
Use: Dessert, culinary
Flesh colour: Medium yellow with slight red pigmentation at the pit.
Stone: Clingstone until the fruit is soft ripe.
Fruit description: The fine-textured flesh is firm with good flavour. The fruit are round and pubescence (peach fuzz) is light and short. Skin colour is 80% to 90% extremely dark red with a bright yellow ground colour. Fruit has very high resistance to flesh browning.
Blossom time: Early September—early October
Ripening times: Early September—early October
Pollination: Self-fertile
Chilling requirements: 850 hours
Other information: Flower buds possess average cold hardiness. Correll exhibits moderate resistance to bacterial spot. It is a consistent producer and heavy thinning is required most years. Many commercial growers have reported problems in obtaining their preferred large fruit size on Correll.

CRESTHAVEN

Provenance: South Haven Experiment Station, Canada.
Use: Dessert and culinary. Excellent for fresh eating and making jams and jellies.
Flesh colour: Yellow
Stone: Freestone
Fruit description: Firm, large fruit. Sweet, juicy reddish-yellow to orange-coloured peaches. Very good flavour.
Blossom time: Early September—early October
Ripening times: Early September—early October
Pollination: While Cresthaven is considered to be somewhat self-pollinating, it tends to set heavier quantities of fruit with a different variety of the same species growing nearby.
Chilling requirements: 850 hours
Other information: Fair tolerance to bacterial spot. Highly ornamental. Cresthaven Peach is covered in stunning clusters of fragrant pink flowers along the branches in early spring, which emerge from rosy flower buds before the leaves emerge. Its dark green foliage turns yellow in autumn. Fruit tends to overset. Susceptible to late spring freezes. Needs full sun and well-drained soil

CURRAEARLY

Blossom time: Early September—early October
Ripening times: Late December
No other information available.

DE WET

Synonyms: De-Wet, Dewet
Provenance: South Africa
Use: Unknown
Flesh colour: Yellow
Stone: Clingstone
Fruit description: Oval shape with point. Yellow skin colour with 75% red.
Blossom time: Unknown
Ripening times: Unknown, but is said to be an early ripener.
Pollination: Unknown
Chilling requirements: Unknown

DESERT GOLD

Synonyms: Desertgold
Provenance: USA
Use: Dessert, culinary
Flesh colour: Yellow to deep orange
Stone: Semi-clingstone
Fruit description: Medium sized, round fruit. Yellow with red blush. Good quality flesh. Tree-ripened fruit has good flavour and sweetness for such an early variety.
Blossom time: Unknown
Ripening times: Very early
Pollination: Self-fertile
Chilling requirements: 200 or fewer hours below 7°C (45°F). Low chilling requirement. Excellent for warmer regions.
Other information: A heavy bearing cultivar. The tree grows up to 9m (30 feet) tall with an equal spread.

It needs full sun and 250 chill hours between 0°C and 7°C (32° and 45° Fahrenheit) to set fruit.

Prunus persica 'Desert Gold'. Photo: Dave Wilson Nursery

DESERT RED

Synonyms: None known
Provenance: Unknown
Use: Dessert, culinary
Flesh colour: Unknown.
Stone: Clingstone
Fruit description: Excellent quality, good colour, firm flesh.
Other information: A heavy cropper, giving a high yield. Produces large fruit when thinned and girdled. Highly susceptible to bacterial spot, high percentage of fused (twin) fruit.

Dixigem

Synonyms: None known

Provenance: The Dixigem peach, introduced in the USA in 1944, is the result of a cross between an unnamed seedling of Dewey X St. John and the South Haven variety. The Dewey X St. John seedling was selected by W. F. Wight during the early years of the peach-breeding work of the United States Department of Agriculture.

Use: Dessert, culinary. Dixigem is also a good variety for canning and freezing. The flesh is nonbrowning—that is, it shows relatively little discolouration when thawed after being frozen. Few varieties possess this character, and it is one that adds greatly to the value of Dixigem for freezing. These characteristics, together with its attractive appearance, firm flesh, and good flavour make this an excellent choice for the home gardener.

Flesh colour: Yellow with little red in the pit cavity.

Stone: semi-clingstone. The flesh adheres to the stone more than that of some of the later ripening varieties, but it separates readily from the stone before the fruit is eating-ripe.

Fruit description: Flesh is firm but melting, fine-textured, juicy and good-flavoured. The fruit is medium-sized and ovate and has light pubescence (fuzz). An attractive, light-red blush covers about half the surface and a bright-yellow ground colours the rest of it. The firm flesh means it can be shipped without risk of bruising, if packed well.

Blossom time: Early September—early October

Ripening times: Mid January—late January

Pollination: Pollen fertile.
Chilling requirements: 850 hours.
Other information: The tree is vigorous, productive, upright to slightly spreading.

DIXIRED

Synonyms: None known
Provenance: The Dixired peach, introduced in the USA in 1945, is a seedling of self-pollinated Halehaven.
Use: Dessert and culinary
Flesh colour: Yellow
Stone: Clingstone
Fruit description: The Dixired fruit is medium-sized, and round. Its pubescence is very light. About three-fourths of the yellow surface is covered with an attractive bright-red blush. The flesh is firm but melting, medium-textured, juicy, subacid to sweet, and good-flavoured. Unusually firm for an early variety, so ships very well.
Blossom time: Early September—early October
Ripening times: Mid December—early January
Pollination: Pollen fertile
Chilling requirements: 950 hours
Other information: The tree is moderately vigorous, productive, upright to somewhat spreading. The fruit attains high colour several days before it is mature. There is danger of picking it too unripe at the shipping-ripe stage, for even at that early stage most of the surface of the fruit is covered with an attractive bright-red blush. Colour develops well on fruit even in shaded portions of the tree.

Doncaster Crawford

Blossom time: Early September—early October
Ripening times: Late February
No other information available.

Dripstone Elberta

Blossom time: Early September—early October
Ripening times: Early February—mid February
    The following advertisement appeared in the Barrier Miner (Broken Hill, NSW: 1888—1954) dated Tuesday 22 August 1950:

```
'SUMMER FRUITS:-PEACHES:
    Hales Early. Wiggins.
      Dripstone Elberta.
        J. H. Hale.'
```

Dwarf Valley Red

Synonyms: Valley Dwarf Red, Super Dwarf Valley Red.
Provenance: Unknown
Use: Dessert, culinary
Flesh colour: Yellow
Stone: Freestone
Fruit description: Size and shape is medium and round to oblong. Skin colour is orange-yellow with a deep red blush. Flesh is golden when ripe and the eating quality is very good, with a melting, sweet flavour.
Blossom time: Unknown.
Ripening times: Mid to late summer
Pollination: Self-fertile
Chilling requirements: High chill. Unsuited to warm climates.
Other information: A hardy, compact tree. First fruit appears when tree is two years old. Grows 2m high x 2m wide.

Heritage Peach Cultivars

―❦―

in Australia
E to G

Prunus Persica

The Florida Peaches

Low Chill Peach and Nectarine Cultivars from the University Of Florida Breeding Program: 50 Years of Progress. State Horticultural Society, 2001.

'The most commonly known peach and nectarine cultivars such as 'Elberta' or 'Redhaven' cannot be grown successfully in mild climates like Florida because they are high-chill cultivars and do not receive enough winter chilling to satisfy dormancy requirements. In fact, prior to 1970 the major impediment toward peach production in subtropical or tropical locations has been the lack of cultivars with adaptation in winter chilling.

'A breeding program was initiated at the University of Florida in the early 1950s to produce early ripening, low-chill, high fruit quality cultivars for adaptability in Florida.

'Forty low chill peach [Prunus persica (L.) Batsch] and nectarine cultivars have been named and released from the University of Florida breeding program since 1950 and many additional clonal selections have been named in other countries. These peaches and nectarines ripen early and target a market window between 15 April and 1 June [in the northern hemisphere].

'The fruit of the more recent releases have significant advantages over earlier releases in terms of earlier ripening, increased size and firmness, rounder shape, and more attractive skin colour.

'Peaches and nectarines can be categorized based on melting and non-melting fruit types. The new generation of peaches and nectarines are the non-melting flesh types. They can be harvested and shipped at physiological maturity since the flesh is firm and it resists bruising.

'The most recent non-melting flesh peaches from the University of Florida breeding program are 'UFGold', 'UF2000', 'UFO', and 'Gulfprince'; 'UFQueen' is the first non-melting flesh nectarine. All the aforementioned cultivars are patented. The melting and non-melting flesh peaches from the University of Florida that are suitable for trial in Florida are as follows: central Florida—'Flordaprince', 'Flordaglo', Tropicbeauty', and Tropicsnow'; north central Florida—'Flordadawn', Flordaking', 'Flordacrest', 'UFGold', 'UF2000', and 'UFO'; and northern Florida—'Flordadawn', 'Flordaking', 'Flordacrest', and 'Gulfprince'.

'Peach and nectarine production in Florida has good potential for expansion because of an excellent market window for fresh fruit during the early to mid-spring. All recent University of Florida cultivars produce fruit that ripen from late April to early June [in the northern hemisphere]. Peach cultivars are now available from the University of Florida breeding program that ripen at least 2-3 weeks earlier than peaches from other regions of the United States.

'All recent cultivars have a low chill requirement (100 to 500 chilling units, or 'cu'), a short fruit development period (60 to 110 days), and good fruit shape, firmness, taste, attractiveness, and resistance to bacterial spot.

'Over the last five years there has been a major shift in emphasis toward the production of non-melting flesh peaches that resist bruising and can be picked at physiological maturity and therefore can be shipped more easily to distant markets.

Internationally, the Florida breeding program is perhaps the best known and most productive of any low chill peach program. Researchers and growers from many countries [including Australia] correspond and visit regularly to seek new budwood and information. Commercial production now occurs in more than 16 countries as a result of this cooperative effort.'

Some low chill Florida cultivars include:

Flordaprince, Tropic Beauty, Tropic Snow, Flordaking, Flordacrest, Flordaglo, Flordagold, Flordastar, Flordagrande, Flordagem, Flordabelle, Newbelle, Shermans Red, Sherman's Early, San Pedro, Maravilha, Flordasun, Flordared, Flordaqueen, Flordahome, Flordabeauty, Flordadawn, Desert Red.

EARLIBELLE

Synonyms: Earli Belle
Provenance: South Africa. Released 1986.
Use: Dessert and culinary
Flesh colour: White
Stone: Clingstone
Fruit description: Diameter 63 mm, ovate in shape, skin colour is red. Soft flesh has a melting texture. Eating quality is moderately good.
Blossom time: Mid August—mid September
Ripening times: Mid late December
Pollination: Self-fertile
Chilling requirements: Medium-low (201 - 400 hours).
Other information: A vigorous tree. Fruit has poor keeping quality and should be used within two weeks.

Prunus persica 'Earlibelle'. Photo: Agricultural Research Council

EARLIGRANDE

Synonyms: Earli Grande

Provenance: Unknown. Use: Dessert, culinary

Flesh colour: Yellow?

Stone: Semi-freestone

Fruit description: Medium to large fruit, yellow skin with a red blush. Firm with excellent flavour.

Blossom time: Mid Aug—mid September

Ripening times: Mid December—late December

Pollination: Self-fertile

Chilling requirements: Very low chill.

Other information: The tree is a heavy producer. Does well in hot summer areas.

Prunus persica 'Earligrande'. Photo: McCabe's Nursery

Earlired

Synonyms: None known
Provenance: Introduced by the USDA (United States Department of Agriculture) in 1960
Use: Dessert and culinary
Flesh colour: Yellow
Stone: Semi-free at the soft-ripe stage.
Fruit description: An attractive fruit, medium in size and well-covered with a bright red blush over a yellow ground colour. Its firm flesh is melting and of good flavour.
Blossom time: Early September—early October
Ripening times: Late December—early January
Pollination: Self-fertile
Chilling requirements: About the same as Elberta.
Other information: The tree is vigorous and annually productive. The fruit require early and heavy thinning. It is moderately susceptible to bacterial leaf spot.

Early O'Henry

Use: Dessert and culinary.
Flesh colour: Yellow
Stone: Freestone
Fruit description: A rounded, well-coloured peach with juicy flesh.
Ripening times: Unknown, but probably earlier than O'Henry.
Pollination: Self-fertile
Chilling requirements: Unknown

Elberta

Synonyms: None known
Provenance: USA, 1950s.
Use: Dessert, culinary. Ideal for eating, juice, drying, stewing and canning.
Flesh colour: Yellow
Stone: Freestone, with the smallest pit-to-fruit ratio of any peach.
Fruit description: A very large peach with excellent eating qualities. Used for fresh fruit, juice, drying and stewing. The skin is red blushed over a deep golden yellow colour. An exceptional wonderfully sweet flavour, said to be one of the sweetest peaches of all.
Blossom time: Unknown
Ripening times: Mid to late season maturity.
Pollination: Self-fertile
Chilling requirements: 850 hours
Other information: The Elberta is the best known yellow canning peach. Tree grows to approximately 4 x 4 metres. Elberta used to be called the 'Queen of Peaches'.

From *Alabama's Changing Peach Industry*, by E.V. Smith (1958):

'Elberta was the leading variety in Alabama in 1957 and has led for several years. However, in recent years there has been an important shift to earlier ripening varieties. Highly favorable prices for early peaches have greatly influenced this shift. For example, there has been a tremendous increase in the acreage devoted to Dixired, an early variety.

The 10 leading varieties of the 49 planted in Alabama commercial orchards in 1957 in order of number of trees were: Elberta, Dixired, Coronet, Redcap, Halehaven, Redhaven, Cardinal, Keystone, Southland, and Hiland. All of the leading ones ripen before or with Elberta, indicating the shift to earlier ripening varieties.'

Ellerbe

Synonyms: Ellerbre
Provenance: Ellerbe resulted from a cross of Pekin x Candor. It was released in the USA in 1975.
Use: Dessert and culinary
Flesh colour: Yellow
Stone: Freestone. The pit is free from the flesh when the fruit is ripe.
Fruit description: Fruits are round to round-oblong with short and sparse pubescence. Ellerbe fruit are similar to those of Winblo except that the ground colour is brighter yellow and it has more red pigmentation around the pit cavity. Fruit size is usually slightly less than that of Winblo under similar crop load conditions. Ellerbe is moderately resistant to flesh browning. and the fruit are very resistant to split-pitting. Flavour is excellent.
Blossom time: Mid September—early October
Ripening times: Mid January—late January
Pollination: Self-fertile
Chilling requirements: 850 hours
Other information: Ellerbe's cropping performance is excellent, with heavy thinning required in most years. Trees of Ellerbe are vigorous, and highly resistant to bacterial spot.

Emery

Synonyms: None known

Provenance: Emery resulted from a cross of Rochester x Red Skin. It was released in the USA in 1968.

Use: Dessert, culinary

Flesh colour: Yellow

Stone: Freestone.

Fruit description: Fruits are round with heavy pubescence. Emery is below average in attractiveness, with 50% of the fruit surface covered with a dull red blush over a dull yellow ground colour. Fruit are medium in size, averaging 6.6 cm (2.5 inches) under full crop conditions. Emery has excellent fruit firmness, and the fruit keep well after harvest. The medium yellow flesh is melting, but it is slightly mealy and dry. Flavour is average. and the fruit are very resistant to split-pitting. The flesh browns readily

Blossom time: Early September—early October

Ripening times: Early September—early October

Pollination: Self-fertile

Chilling requirements: 900 hours

Other information: Crop production is excellent and thinning is necessary in most years. Fruit keeps well after harvest. Emery is resistant to bacterial spot.

Erly-Red-Fre

Synonyms: Erly Red Fre

Provenance: USA, 1938. W.M. Perry, Chase City, Virginia, and Bountiful Ridge Nurseries, Princess Anne, Maryland, from a chance seedling.

Use: Dessert, culinary

Flesh colour: White

Stone: Semi-freestone

Fruit description: A large peach of good eating quality. Fruit is attractive with bright red blush on creamy white background

Blossom time: Early September—early October

Ripening times: Early January—mid January

Pollination: Self-fertile

Chilling requirements: 850 hours

Other information: The tree is vigorous, hardy and a heavy bearer. Moderately resistant to peach spot.

Prunus persica 'Erly-Red-Fre'. Photos: bib.ge

FAIRHAVEN

Synonyms: Fair Haven
Provenance: South Haven, Michigan, USA.
Use: Dessert and culinary. This variety shows good resistance to browning and that makes it a good selection for freezing and canning.
Flesh colour: Yellow
Stone: Freestone
Fruit description: Medium fruit with red-cheeked and dotted red yellow skin; very firm, juicy flesh with good flavour.
Blossom time: Mid September—early October
Ripening times: Mid January—late January
Pollination: Self-fertile.
Chilling requirements: Unknown

Prunus persica 'Fairhaven'

FAIRTIME

Synonyms: None known
Provenance: California
Use: Dessert and culinary. An excellent freezer or fresh-eating selection.
Flesh colour: Yellow
Stone: Freestone
Fruit description: An attractive yellow skin and bright red blush where exposed to sun. Delicious. Well-balanced flavour. Very large—average diameter 7cm (3") to 9cm (3-1/2". A highly esteemed peach.
Blossom time: Early September—early October
Ripening times: Early March—mid March. One of the last peaches to ripen.
Pollination: Self-fertile
Chilling requirements: 700-800 hours below 7°C (45°F)

Prunus persica 'Fairtime'. Photo: Dave Wilson Nursery

Fairway

Synonyms: None known
Use: Dessert and culinary.
Blossom time: Early September—late September
Ripening times: Mid January—early February

Favorita I

Synonyms: Possibly 'Favorita Morettini I'?
Provenance: Italy
Use: Dessert and culinary.
Blossom time: Early September—early October
Ripening times: Mid December—late December

Favorita II

Synonyms: None known
Provenance: Italy
Use: Dessert and culinary.
Blossom time: Early September—early October
Ripening times: Mid December—late December

Fay 3

Synonyms: None known
Use: Dessert and culinary.
Blossom time: Early September—early October
Ripening times: Mid February—late February

Fay 4

Synonyms: None known
Use: Dessert and culinary.
Blossom time: Mid September—early October
Ripening times: Mid February

Fay Elberta

Synonyms: Faye Elberta
Provenance: USA
Use: Dessert and culinary
Flesh colour: Yellow
Stone: Freestone
Fruit description: Medium to large, yellow skin peach with little red blush, that has fairly good shape and good flavour. Flesh is fine-grained with good firmness. Similar to Elberta, but blooms earlier and ripens 1 to 6 days after Elberta. Has more red blush on skin than 'Elberta'. Good for shipping and canning.
Blossom time: Late August—early October
Ripening times: Mid February—late February
Pollination: Self-fertile
Chilling requirements: 750 hours
Other information: Colourful flowers. Very popular peach for all uses. A midseason ripener that keeps better than 'Elberta'. Bears large, colourful, single flowers. 'Fantastic Elberta' is a double-flowered sport of this cultivar and its fruit too, has excellent flavour.

Fayette

Synonyms: None known
Provenance: USA
Use: Dessert and culinary
Flesh colour: Yellow
Stone: Freestone
Fruit description: A very large, round peach. This late season peach has smooth, deep red skin with some yellow-orange shades and a sweet taste.
Blossom time: Early September—late September
Ripening times: Early February—mid February
Pollination: Self-fertile.
Chilling requirements: 850 hours
Other information: Heavy cropper. Needs thinning. Fayette tree grows vigorously and flowers profusely and guarantees heavy crop every year.

Prunus persica 'Fayette'. Photo: Milan Havlis Garden Centre

FERTILA MORETTINI

Synonyms: Fertilia L Morettini
Provenance: Introduced by A. Morettini (see endnotes) in Italy in 1959. One of the parents is J. H. Hale.
Use: Dessert and culinary
Flesh colour: Unknown but probably yellow.
Stone: Unknown
Fruit description: Stunning red skin, medium to large fruit with a round shape and short, soft pubescence (fuzz).
Blossom time: Early September—early October
Ripening times: Late December—early January
Pollination: Self-fertile
Chilling requirements: Unknown
Other information: In the 1950s, peach breeder A. Morettini, also introduced 'La Precocissima', 'La Gialla di Firenze', 'Morettini No. 1', 'Morettini No. 2', 'Prodigiosa Morettini' and 'Gialla Precoce Morettini.'

FIRE PRINCE

Synonyms: None known
Provenance: USA
Use: Dessert and culinary
Flesh colour: Unknown
Stone: Freestone
Fruit description: A flavourful peach having beautiful red colour. 90% red, firm and good for shipping.
Blossom time: Early September—early October
Ripening times: Unknown
Pollination: Self-fertile
Chilling requirements: 750 hours
Other information: None known

Flamecrest

Synonyms: Flame Crest
Provenance: USA
Use: Dessert and culinary
Flesh colour: Yellow
Stone: Freestone
Fruit description: The fruit is large and bright red on a yellow background, with short fuzz and a very round, firm shape. The flesh has an excellent texture and superb flavour, especially when eaten straight after being picked off the tree.
Blossom time: Early September—early October
Ripening times: Mid January—early February
Pollination: Self-fertile
Chilling requirements: Unknown
Other information: 'Flame Crest' is one of the better old-fashioned later ripening peaches. This variety usually yields a larger crop than other varieties and produces an unusually large peach for such a large crop. The tree grows best in a sunny, sheltered position in loamy, free-draining soils.

Prunus persica 'Flamecrest', Photo: Edible Gardens, New Zealand.

Flavorcrest

Synonyms: Flavor Crest, Flavourcrest
Provenance: USA
Use: Dessert and culinary
Flesh colour: Yellow
Stone: Semi-freestone
Fruit description: Medium to large, bright red skin over bright yellow background, skin not very fuzzy. Fruit is large, round, with flesh that is exceptionally firm, smooth-textured, sweet and highly-flavoured. Prone to splitstone/split pit under drought conditions.
Blossom time: Early September—late September
Ripening times: Early January—mid January
Pollination: Self-fertile
Chilling requirements: 750 hours
Other information: Appears to be winter bud hardy. Heavy fruit set. Good shipper.

Flordabeauty

Synonyms: None known
Provenance: One of the low-chill cultivars bred by Florida University, USA.
Use: Dessert and culinary
Flesh colour: Unknown
Stone: Unknown
Fruit description: Skin has a green background colour.
Blossom time: Unknown
Ripening times: Unknown
Pollination: self-fertile
Chilling requirements: Unknown
Other information: None known

FLORDABELLE

Synonyms: Florda Belle, Florida Belle.

Provenance: One of the low-chill cultivars bred by Florida University, USA.

Use: Dessert and culinary

Flesh colour: Yellow

Stone: Freestone

Fruit description: Large fruit with a beautifully round shape, firm flesh and excellent flavour. The fruit colour is 80% red over a yellow ground, very attractive. Flesh does not brown much.

Blossom time: Early Aug—mid September

Ripening times: Mid January

Pollination: Self-fertile

Chilling requirements: 200-250 hours—moderately low chill.

Other information: A older variety with excellent flavour and disease resistance. Melting flesh. Quite good resistance to bacterial spot.

Prunus persica 'Flordabelle'. Photo: Chestnut Hill Tree Farm

FLORDACREST

Synonyms: Florda Crest, Florida Crest.

Provenance: One of the low-chill cultivars bred by Florida University, USA.

Use: Dessert and culinary

Flesh colour: Yellow

Stone: Semi-freestone

Fruit description: Melting flesh. A sweet, excellent tasting attractively peach with red skin on a yellow background.

Blossom time: Unknown

Ripening times: Early ripening

Pollination: Self-fertile

Chilling requirements: Low chill

Prunus persica 'Flordacrest'. Photo: Chestnut Hill Tree Farm

Flordagem

Synonyms: Florda Gem, Florida Gem
Provenance: One of the low-chill cultivars bred by Florida University, USA.
Use: Dessert and culinary, including distilling.
Flesh colour: Yellow
Stone: Semi-freestone
Fruit description: medium sized, round fruit, coloured red over bright yellow, very attractive, firm flesh with excellent flavour, flesh does not brown easily, short fuzz on skin.
Blossom time: Unknown
Ripening times: Unknown
Pollination: Self-fertile
Chilling requirements: 250 hours
Other information: Moderate resistance to bacterial spot.

Flordaglo

Synonyms: Flordaglow, Florda Glow, Florda Glo.
Provenance: One of the low-chill cultivars bred by Florida University, USA.
Use: Dessert and culinary
Flesh colour: White
Stone: Unknown
Fruit description: Fruit is large for the season, with sweet, melting, firm, non-browning flesh.
Blossom time: Unknown
Ripening times: Unknown

Pollination: Self fertile
Chilling requirements: 150 hours (low chill)
Other information: Gives a high crop yield.

FLORDAGOLD

Synonyms: Fordagold, Floragold, Florda Gold
Provenance: Bred by Florida University, USA, but not low-chill.
Use: Dessert and culinary
Flesh colour: Yellow
Stone: Semi-freestone
Fruit description: Flordagold sets the standard for firmness, size and attractiveness in its season, with highly coloured fruit and excellent flavour.
Blossom time: Mid August—mid September
Ripening times: Mid December—early January
Pollination: Self fertile
Chilling requirements: Requires up to 325 hours chill.
Other information: High flower bud set. Susceptible to bacterial spot.

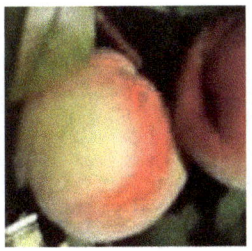

Prunus persica 'Flordagold'. Photo: Olea Nurseries

FLORDAGRANDE

Synonyms: Florda Grand, Florda Grande.

Provenance: Released by the University of Florida, USA, in 1984.

Use: Dessert and culinary

Flesh colour: Yellow

Stone: Semi-freestone

Fruit description: Bears large fruit with good colour. Good overall quality. Softens quickly.

Blossom time: Unknown

Ripening times: Unknown

Pollination: Self fertile

Chilling requirements: very low. Requires 75 or fewer chill hours. Suits sub-tropical environments.

Prunus persica 'Flordagrande'

FLORDAHOME

Synonyms: Florda Home
Provenance: Released by the University of Florida, USA
Use: Dessert and culinary
Flesh colour: White
Stone: Unknown
Fruit description: Very nice quality, sweet, smooth-textured, soft flesh, juicy, flavourful.
Blossom time: Early September—early October
Ripening times: Early—mid January
Pollination: Self fertile
Chilling requirements: Unknown
Other information: A double pink flowering ornamental peach. It is reported to be fairly resistant to nematodes.

FLORDAKING

Synonyms: Florda King
Provenance: Flordaking was developed by the University of Florida, USA.
Use: Dessert and culinary
Flesh colour: Yellow
Stone: Clingstone or semi-freestone
Fruit description: Large size for an early peach, and has a beautiful red blush over a yellow base colour. Soft, melting flesh.
Blossom time: Late August—mid September
Ripening times: Mid—late December
Pollination: Self fertile
Chilling requirements: 300—400 chill hours.

Other information: Produces abundant crops of good flavoured peaches. Many split pits if crop load is not high. Fruit are pointed in shape if chilling is inadequate.

Prunus persica 'Flordaking'. Photo: Chestnut Hill Tree Farm

FLORDAPRINCE

Synonyms: Florda Prince, Florida Prince, Floraprince.
Provenance: Developed by the University of Florida, USA.
Use: Dessert and culinary
Flesh colour: Yellow
Stone: Semi-freestone
Fruit description: A medium sized round fruit. Firm flesh is covered by a beautiful deep red-blushed skin.
Blossom time: Early August—early September
Ripening times: Mid—late December
Pollination: Self fertile
Chilling requirements: 150 hours.

Other information: Earliest fruiting peach, popular low chill variety. Flordaprince sets the standard for early-ripening peaches, but susceptible to bacterial spot. Early-ripening Flordastar replaces Flordaprince in areas where bacterial spot is a problem.

Prunus persica 'Flordaprince'. Photo: Florida Gardener.

FLORDAQUEEN

Synonyms: Florida Queen, Florda Queen.

Provenance: Requiring scant chilling to make good crops, this University of Florida introduction is heralded for its high heat and humidity tolerance. First made available in the 1960s, it was bred primarily for the North Florida peach industry, but is not as widely grown today.

Use: Dessert and culinary. Good for fresh eating as well as canning and cooking.

Flesh colour: Yellow

Stone: Semi-freestone
Fruit description: Medium-sized peaches. The yellow, red-blushed fruits have reasonably firm flesh.
Blossom time: Late August—late September
Ripening times: Early—mid January
Pollination: Self fertile
Chilling requirements: Low chill.
Other information: None known.

Flordared

Synonyms: Florda Red, Florida Red
Provenance: One of the peach varieties developed at the Florida Agricultural Experiment Station, Flordared was derived from selection and open pollination over four generations from an original hybridization of Southland x Hawaiian.
Use: Dessert and culinary
Flesh colour: White
Stone: Freestone
Fruit description: Fruit is of good quality, though it lacks firmness and red overcolour.
Blossom time: Late August—mid September
Ripening times: Mid January
Pollination: Self fertile
Chilling requirements: This cultivar has very low winter chilling requirement, estimated at 50 to 100 hours below 7°C (45° F).
Other information: The trees are vigourous and tend to grow willowy. The tree flowers very early and is subject to late-spring frost damage

Flordastar

Synonyms: Florda Star
Provenance: Florida Agricultural Experiment Station, USA.
Use: Dessert and culinary
Flesh colour: Yellow
Stone: Semi-freestone
Fruit description: A medium sized round fruit. Firm flesh is covered by a blushing skin.
Blossom time: Early August—early September
Ripening times: Mid—late December
Pollination: Self fertile
Chilling requirements: 150 hours.
Other information: Flordastar is an-early ripening, low chill cultivar that can be used to replace Flordaprince in areas where bacterial spot is a problem.

Flordasun

Synonyms: Florda Sun, Florida Sun
Provenance: Florida Agricultural Experiment Station, USA.
Use: Dessert and culinary
Flesh colour: Unknown
Stone: Unknown
Fruit description: Large, red skin.
Blossom time: Mid August—mid September
Ripening times: Mid December
Pollination: Self fertile
Chilling requirements: Low chill
Other information: None known

Fragar

Synonyms: None known
Provenance: Unknown
Use: Dessert and culinary
Flesh colour: White
Stone: Clingstone
Fruit description: Fragar produces medium to large sized oblong fruits. With a firm but melting flesh, this fruit needs to be handled with care as bruising occurs easily. A beautiful peach, with pink to red skin over a greeny cream background. Flesh is softer and coarser than Tasty Zee, but with more complex flavour.
Blossom time: Early—late September
Ripening times: Mid—late February
Pollination: Self fertile
Chilling requirements: Unknown
Other information: Requires hot weather during its growing season and a moist well drained soil.

Frome

Blossom time: Late August—late September
Ripening times: Late February—early March

Galston Red

Blossom time: Early September—early October
Ripening times: Late December—early January

GARNET BEAUTY

Synonyms: None known

Provenance: Discovered in 1951 by Mr. Bruner and jointly released with the Harrow Research Centre (Canada). Released in 1958 by Garnet Bruner and Agriculture Canada. At the height of its popularity this bud sport of Redhaven ranked second in number of trees to its parent in Ontario, Canada.

Use: Dessert and culinary. It is good for canning and freezing

Flesh colour: Yellow

Stone: Semi-freestone

Fruit description: A good-quality peach, attractive, usually not subject to split-pit/splitstone. Medium to large, slightly elongated, almost fuzzless, red fruit, similar to its parent, Redhaven. Firm flesh streaked with red. Smooth fine texture.

Blossom time: Early/Mid September—early October

Ripening times: Late December—early January

Pollination: Self fertile

Chilling requirements: 850 hours

Other information: Quite bud-hardy to cold temperatures.

Prunus persica 'Garnet Beauty'. Photo: Pete's Produce Farm

Glenalton

Synonyms: Glen Alton
Provenance: Selected in Australia, at Glenalton, New South Wales, late 1960s.
Use: Dessert and culinary. Good for bottling.
Flesh colour: Yellow
Stone: Freestone
Fruit description: The skin is red, the fruit is medium sized.
Blossom time: Early—late September
Ripening times: Mid—late February
Pollination: Self fertile
Chilling requirements: Unknown
Other information: A heavy cropper.

Glohaven

Synonyms: Glow Haven, Glo Haven
Provenance: South Haven, USA
Use: Dessert and culinary. Firm yellow flesh is resistant to browning. Superior canning and freezing qualities.
Flesh colour: Yellow
Stone: Freestone
Fruit description: Large nearly round, attractive fruit. Very tough, mostly red skin is practically fuzzless with a deep yellow ground colour.
Blossom time: Mid September—early October
Ripening times: Mid January—early February
Pollination: Self fertile
Chilling requirements: 850 hours
Other information: The tree is vigorous and productive. Excellent quality fruit for fresh market and commercial processing. Keeps and ships very well.

Golden Amber

Blossom time: Late August—mid/late September
Ripening times: Late December—mid January

Golden Gem

Blossom time: Early September—early October
Ripening times: Late December—early January

Golden Queen

Synonyms: None known
Provenance: A well known heritage variety from New Zealand.
Use: Dessert and culinary. Used for fresh fruit, and in preserves, and the most popular variety for canning and bottling.
Flesh colour: Yellow
Stone: Clingstone
Fruit description: Medium sized fruit, rich orange-golden skin and sweet, firm, juicy, deep orange flesh with a good flavour.
Blossom time: Unknown
Ripening times: Mid March to early April (very late season).
Pollination: Self fertile
Chilling requirements: Unknown
Other information: Also used as a rootstock. Trees may need staking when young as they crop very heavily.

Golden Red

Blossom time: Mid September—early October
Ripening times: Mid—late December

Greys

This peach cultivar is recorded as having been grown at the Bathurst Primary Industries Centre in Australia. No other information is available.

Guame Cling

This cultivar is recorded as being grown by members of The Rare Fruit Society of South Australia. No other information is available.

Heritage Peach Cultivars

in Australia
H to K

Prunus Persica

The Harrow Peaches

From: *Genetic Improvement of Peach, Nectarine and Apricot Cultivars and Rootstocks for Canada*, by R.E.C. Layne (1996).

'Ontario leads Canada in both peach and nectarine production with 82 per cent.

'A breeding program to improve peach, nectarine and apricot cultivars and rootstocks was initiated in the early 1960s at the Harrow Research Station, in southwestern Ontario. Major breeding objectives included the genetic improvement of cold hardiness, late blooming, tree vigour, annual productivity, natural central leader growth habit, precocity, uniformity of ripening and freedom from major disorders including preharvest fruit drop, split pits, and skin cracking.

'Other character of importance included disease resistance, especially to perennial canker, bacterial spot and brown rot.

'Important fruit characteristics for improvement included extension of harvest season from early to late, improvement of fruit size, skin colour, flesh firmness, freeness, sweetness, juiciness, and extension of shelf life.

'Rootstock breeding objectives have emphasized cold hardiness, disease resistance, high seed productivity, good seed germination, compatibility with a wide range of scion cultivars, freedom from suckering, and adaptation to sandy loam and clay loam soils.

'This research has led to the introduction of:

'Ten yellow-fleshed, cold hardy, disease resistant, peach cultivars for the fresh market, ('Harbelle', 'Canadian Harmony', 'Harbrite', 'Harken', 'Harbinger', 'Harland', 'Harson', 'Harrow Beauty', 'Harcrest', 'Harrow Diamond');

'Three cold hardy ornamental peach cultivars ('Harrow Candifloss', 'Harrow Frostipink', 'Harrow Rubirose');

'Two hardy rootstock seed sources for peach and nectarine ('Harrow Blood', 'Siberian C');

Three attractive, disease resistant, cold hardy, nectarines ('Harko', 'Hardired', 'Harblaze');

'Seven cold hardy, disease resistant, high quality, apricot cultivars ('Harcot', 'Harogem', 'Hargrand', 'Harlayne', 'Harglow', 'Laycot', 'Harval');

'A highly productive, rootstock seed source for apricot ('Haggith').'

[There are also two other cultivars called 'Harrow Fair' and 'Harrow Dawn'.]

'Collectively, these cultivar and rootstock introductions have had a major impact on the Canadian fruit industry.

'In addition, some of these introductions are being commercially grown in other countries [such as Australia] and used as parents by other Prunus breeders, especially as genetic resources for improving cold hardiness, disease resistance and fruit quality.'

The Haven Peaches

Stanley Johnstone was the son of an agricultural extension agent in Michigan, Canada. He held the position of Superintendent of the South Haven Experiment Station from 1920 to 1969.

Stanley had no training in genetics but he realised what kind of peaches the market demanded. Perceiving that the local peach farmers grew too much 'Elberta', resulting in a market glut when they all ripened at the same time, he decided to try breeding firm, red peaches that would mature earlier than 'Elberta'. He planted some J.H. Hale peach pits and waited for them to bear fruit. His first seedling selections resulted in the release of 'Halehaven' in 1932 and 'Kalhaven' in 1938.

Crossing 'Halehaven' with 'Kalhaven' resulted in 'Redhaven' which, when it was released it 1940, was the first good quality freestone peach available to consumers. It rapidly became popular in high-chill regions because it is a prolifically-bearing tree with firm, attractive fruit. At one time it was the most widely-grown peach in the world.

'Until the Redhaven peach came along in 1940, Elberta held the title as the most-planted peach variety in the world.

'According to Michigan State University cherry breeder Amy Iezzoni, "Before Redhaven appeared, the perfect peach color was a golden undercolor with 25% red blush. Redhaven, the first of the red-skinned peach cultivars, set a new standard for peach color and commanding premium prices.

'By modern standards, however, Redhaven isn't all that red. "Redhaven does not have enough red coloration in some years to compete on the wholesale market," said Bill Shane, who is Michigan State University's current peach breeder.

Source: *Last Bite.* Good Fruit Grower (April 2011)

Later Michigan releases included 'Fairhaven, 'Sunhaven', 'Richaven', 'Glohaven' and 'Cresthaven'.

Halehaven

Synonyms: Hale Haven

Provenance: A hybrid cross between J.H. Hale and South Haven. Origin: USA, 1968,

Use: Dessert and culinary. Eat fresh or use in salads, pies and preserves.

Flesh colour: Yellow

Stone: Freestone

Fruit description: Medium- to large-sized peaches have red skin that turns yellow as the fruits ripen. Good appearance and flavour.

Blossom time: Early September—early October

Ripening times: Mid January—late January

Pollination: Self fertile

Chilling requirements: 850 hours

Other information: none available

Prunus persica 'Halehaven'. Photo: Homeguides

Harbelle

Synonyms: None known
Provenance: A seedling or sport of Sunhaven.
Use: Dessert and culinary
Flesh colour: Yellow
Stone: semi-freestone
Fruit description: none available
Blossom time: Mid September—early October
Ripening times: Mid February—early March
Pollination: Self fertile
Chilling requirements: 850 hours
Other information: none known

Harbinger

Synonyms: None known
Provenance: Unknown
Use: Dessert and culinary
Flesh colour: Yellow
Stone: Clingstone
Fruit description: Colour is 80% bright red over a yellow ground colour. Good flavour.
Blossom time: Late August—late September
Ripening times: Mid December—late December (an early ripener)
Pollination: Self fertile
Chilling requirements: 850 hours
Other information: A good quality extra early peach. The tree is hardy and productive. A clingstone with very few split pits.

Harbrite

Synonyms: None known

Provenance: Released by Agriculture Canada, Harrow Station.

Use: Dessert and culinary. Excellent for freezing and canning.

Flesh colour: Yellow

Stone: Freestone

Fruit description: Medium to large round, attractive fruit with red skin and orange-yellow flesh deepening to red at the pit.

Blossom time: Mid September—early October

Ripening times: Early January—mid January

Pollination: Self fertile

Chilling requirements: 850 hours

Other information: Good winter hardiness, and the fruit are resistant to bacterial spot and brown rot.

Prunus persica 'Harbrite'. Photo: Bylands Nurseries

Harken

Synonyms: None known

Provenance: From Canada; a sibling of Canadian Harmony peach.

Use: Dessert and culinary. Because it oxidizes slowly, Harken freezes well

Flesh colour: Yellow

Stone: Freestone

Fruit description: The large, attractive peach has a good red colour covering most of its surface and a bright yellow ground-colour. The flesh is firm, sweet and of good quality.

Blossom time: Early September—early October

Ripening times: Early—mid January

Pollination: Self fertile

Chilling requirements: 850 hours

Other information: A heavy cropper. Resistance to bacterial spot and brown rot is good.

Prunus persica 'Harken'. Photo: Dave Wilson Nursery

Haruko

Synonyms: Harkuko
Provenance: Japan
Use: Dessert and culinary
Flesh colour: Unknown
Stone: Unknown
Fruit description: none available
Blossom time: Mid September—early October
Ripening times: Mid January—late January
Pollination: Unknown
Chilling requirements: Unknown
Other information: none available

Harmony

Synonyms: Possibly confused with 'Canadian Harmony'?
Provenance: Unknown
Use: Dessert and culinary. Slow to brown. Good freezer.
Flesh colour: Yellow
Stone: Freestone
Fruit description: Medium to large, round, yellow fruit blushed with red. Moderately firm, flesh, slightly red at the pit.
Blossom time: Mid September—early October
Ripening times: Mid January—early February
Pollination: Self fertile
Chilling requirements: Unknown
Other information: Vigorous, upright, spreading tree.

Harrow

Synonyms: None known
Provenance: Harrow Research Station, in southwestern Ontario, Canada.
Use: Dessert and culinary. Good for fresh eating. The low oxidizing flesh means this peach is also excellent for cooking, canning and bottling.
Flesh colour: Yellow
Stone: Semi-freestone. Almost freestone when ripe.
Fruit description: Medium sized attractive fruit with red blush over yellow skin. The pit is resistant to splitting. Deep yellow flesh is of good quality.
Blossom time: Unknown
Ripening times: Unknown
Pollination: Self fertile
Chilling requirements: high chill?
Other information: none available.

Havis

This peach cultivar is recorded as having been grown at the Bathurst Primary Industries Centre in Australia. Chilling requirements: 850 hours. No other information is available.

Hiland

Synonyms: Possibly confused with 'Hyland's Peach'?
Blossom time: Early—late September
Ripening times: Late December—mid January
Other information: This cultivar is recorded as having been grown at the Bathurst Primary Industries Centre in Australia.

Honey Dew Hale

Synonyms: Honeydew Hale
Provenance: USA. Probably Hale Orchards.
Use: Dessert and culinary
Flesh colour: White
Stone: Freestone
Fruit description: Large fruit. Honey Dew Hale peaches are the only variety of white peaches that have a streak of yellow at the seam that goes all the way through the fruit.
Blossom time: Early/Mid September—early October
Ripening times: Early—mid February
Pollination: Self fertile
Chilling requirements: Unknown
Other information: none known

Idlewild

This peach cultivar is recorded as having been grown at the Bathurst Primary Industries Centre in Australia. Chilling requirements: 550 hours.

Inquee

Another Bathurst cultivar.
Blossom time: Late August—mid September
Ripening times: Late December—mid January

Ireland's Peach

Another Bathurst cultivar.
Blossom time: Early—late September
Ripening times: Mid January

J H Hale

Synonyms: Million Dollar Peach, Hale

Provenance: J.H. Hale is an old-time heritage/heirloom cultivar, and still one of the best. J.H. Hale Orchards began in Glastenbury, Connecticutt, USA in 1866, when John Howard Hale and his brother, George, cultivated their grandfather's seven peach trees.

Use: Dessert and culinary. An excellent peach for eating fresh, canning, drying or stewing.

Flesh colour: Yellow

Stone: Freestone

Fruit description: A very large, uniformly round peach with golden-yellow skin overlaid with a crimson blush. Skin is smooth and almost fuzzless. Flesh has a firm texture. J. H. Hale has a wonderfully sweet flavour and aroma.

Blossom time: Early September—early October

Ripening times: Mid—late February

Pollination: J.H. Hale is not fully self fertile—it benefits from cross pollination by an Elberta, Blackburn Elberta or Rio Oso Gem.

Chilling requirements: 850 hours

Other information: Trees grow approximately 4 x 4 metres. Winter tender. Consistent producer; requires good soil. The fruit keeps very well. An outstanding handling and shipping peach, as it does not bruise easily.

J H Hale Hitchcock

This peach cultivar is recorded as having been grown at the Bathurst Primary Industries Centre in Australia.
Blossom time: Mid September—early October
Ripening times: Mid—late February

Jersey Queen

Recorded as having been grown at the Bathurst Primary Industries Centre in Australia.
Blossom time: Early/Mid September—early October
Ripening times: Mid—late February
Chilling requirements: 850 hours

Julie

Recorded as having been grown at the Bathurst Primary Industries Centre in Australia.
Blossom time: Early September—late September
Ripening times: Late February—early March

July Elberta

Synonyms: None known.
Provenance: Developed by Luther Burbank[1]

---

[1] *Luther Burbank (7 March 1849 – 11 April 1926), was an American botanist, horticulturist and a pioneer in agricultural science. He developed more than 800 strains and varieties of plants over his 55-year career. Burbank's varied creations included fruits, flowers, grains, grasses, and vegetables. He developed a spineless cactus (useful for cattle-feed) and the plumcot. Burbank's most successful strains and varieties include the Shasta daisy, the Fire poppy, the July Elberta peach, the Santa Rosa plum, the Flaming Gold nectarine, the Wickson plum, the*

Use: Dessert and culinary
Flesh colour: Yellow
Stone: Freestone
Fruit description: With an attractive, bright red skin, July Elberta is sweet and flavoursome.
Blossom time: Early September—early October
Ripening times: Mid January
Pollination: Self fertile
Chilling requirements: Heat-tolerant, so possibly low-chill.
Other information: Features a very small pit-to-fruit ratio. A highly ornamental tree with clouds of fragrant red blossoms in spring.

Prunus persica 'July Elberta'. Photo: Stark Bros Nurseries

Freestone peach, and the white blackberry. A natural genetic variant of the Burbank potato with russet-coloured skin later became known as the Russet Burbank potato. This large, brown-skinned, white-fleshed potato has become the world's predominant potato in food processing.

Source: 'Luther Burbank' Wikipedia. Accessed 2013.

June Lady

Synonyms: None known

Provenance: Unknown

Use: Dessert and culinary. Delicious eaten fresh or sliced on desserts or breakfasts.

Also excellent for jams and preserves.

Flesh colour: Yellow

Stone: Freestone

Fruit description: A large and flavoursome fruit that benefits from tree ripening. Beautiful bright red and gold skin. Very sweet, but flavour is very well balanced in sweetness and tartness. Flesh is deep yellowy-orange.

Blossom time: Early September—early October

Ripening times: Mid—late January

Pollination: Self fertile

Chilling requirements: Unknown

Other information: none available

Prunus persica 'June Lady. Photo: Hawkes Bay Clean

June Prince

Synonyms: None known
Provenance: Unknown
Use: Dessert and culinary. Excellent for canning whole.
Flesh colour: Unknown
Stone: Clingstone
Fruit description: Small in size. Flesh is very firm.
Blossom time: Early—late September
Ripening times: Late December—early January
Pollination: Self fertile
Chilling requirements: 650 hours
Other information: none known

Kalhaven

Synonyms: Kalehaven
Provenance: Originated in South Haven, Michigan, USA, by the Michigan (South Haven) Agricultural Experiment Station. Introduced commercially in 1936. J.H. Hale x Kalamazoo; cross made in 1924,
Use: Dessert and culinary
Flesh colour: Yellow
Stone: Freestone
Fruit description: Excellent quality, flesh is firm
Blossom time: Early September—late September
Ripening times: Mid—late February. Fruit matures 4 to 7 days before Elberta, helping to fill in the season between Halehaven and Elberta.
Pollination: Self fertile
Chilling requirements: 950 hours
Other information: Ships well. Most nearly resembles J.H. Hale but smaller in size.

Keystone

Recorded as having been grown at the Bathurst Primary Industries Centre in Australia.
Blossom time: Early September—late September
Ripening times: Mid January—early February
Chilling requirements: 750 hours

Kingston

Rootstock. Recorded as having been grown at the Bathurst Primary Industries Centre in Australia.

Kirkman

Recorded as having been grown at the Bathurst Primary Industries Centre in Australia.
Blossom time: Early September—early October
Ripening times: Mid March—late March

Klamt

Synonyms: Klampt
Provenance: Unknown
Use: Dessert and culinary
Flesh colour: Unknown
Stone: Clingstone
Fruit description: Large fruit. Fruit may lack good colour and firmness in some years.
Blossom time: Early September—late September
Ripening times: not available

Heritage Peach Cultivars

---ᴏ⚜ᴏ---

in Australia

L to O

Prunus Persica

La Feliciana

Synonyms: La Feliciano

Provenance: Developed by the Louisana State University in the USA.

Use: Dessert and culinary

Flesh colour: Yellow

Stone: Freestone

Fruit description: Medium to large, round. Dark red blush on skin. Firm, excellent texture and sweet, tangy flavour. Yellow with red flecks in flesh.

Blossom time: Early September—late September

Ripening times: Late-ripening.

Pollination: Self fertile

Chilling requirements: 550-600 chill hours

Other information: Great peach for mild winter areas. Very heavy producer. Tolerant to bacteriosis and brown rot.

Prunus persica 'La Feliciana'. Photo: Lowes

La Gem

Recorded as having been grown at the Bathurst Primary Industries Centre in Australia.
Blossom time: Early September—early October
Ripening times: Early—mid January

La Gold

Recorded as having been grown at the Bathurst Primary Industries Centre in Australia.
Blossom time: Early—late September
Ripening times: Mid—late January
Chilling requirements: 700 hours

La Premier

Recorded as having been grown at the Bathurst Primary Industries Centre in Australia.
Stone: Freestone
Blossom time: Early September—early October
Ripening times: Mid—late January
Chilling requirements: 900 hours

La Red

Recorded as having been grown at the Bathurst Primary Industries Centre in Australia.
Blossom time: Mid September—early October
Ripening times: Mid January—early February

Late Hale

Recorded as having been grown at the Bathurst Primary Industries Centre in Australia.
Blossom time: Early September—early October
Ripening times: Mid February

Late Italian Red

Synonyms: Riverside.
Provenance: Italy?
Use: Dessert and culinary
Flesh colour: Yellow
Stone: Clingstone
Fruit description: Large, round fruit. The skin has a deep red blush over green-yellow background. Flesh is firm; juicy and sweet, with excellent flavour.
Blossom time: Unknown
Ripening times: Unknown
Pollination: Self fertile
Chilling requirements: Unknown
Other information: Useful because of its lateness.

Prunus persica 'Late Italian Red'. Photo: Balhanna Nurseries

Late Loring

Recorded as having been grown at the Bathurst Primary Industries Centre in Australia.
Blossom time: Mid September—early October
Ripening times: Mid January—early February

Late Loring Thomas

Recorded as having been grown at the Bathurst Primary Industries Centre in Australia.
Blossom time: Early September—early October
Ripening times: Late January—early February

Le Vainquer ('The Winner')

Recorded as having been grown at the Bathurst Primary Industries Centre in Australia.
Blossom time: Early September—early October
Ripening times: Mid December

Loring

Synonyms: None known
Provenance: USA
Use: Dessert and culinary. Excellent for drying.
Flesh colour: Yellow
Stone: Freestone
Fruit description: Very large yellow peach with firm yellow flesh and a scarlet blush covering half of its golden yellow skin. A favourite peach in colder regions, excellent flavour and texture.
Blossom time: Early September—early October
Ripening times: Mid January—early February (late season)

Pollination: Self fertile
Chilling requirements: 750 hours
Other information: Reliable cropper. Known for its good quality, Loring lacks hardiness in very cold (snowy) winters. Once an industry standard, it lacks sufficient red skin colour to compete with newer cultivars but its flavour and other qualities make it well worth including in the home orchard.

Madison

Recorded as having been grown at the Bathurst Primary Industries Centre in Australia.
Use: Dessert and culinary
Flesh colour: Deep yellow
Stone: Freestone
Blossom time: Mid September—early October
Ripening times: Early—mid February
Pollination: Self fertile
Chilling requirements: 850 hours

Prunus persica 'Madison'.

Maravilha

Synonyms: None known.
Provenance: A dessert cultivar released by the University of Florida, USA, in 1975.
Use: Dessert and culinary
Flesh colour: White
Stone: Unknown
Fruit description: Fruit round, with red skin. Flesh has a soft, melting texture.
Blossom time: Mid Aug—mid September
Ripening times: Mid—late December
Pollination: Self fertile
Chilling requirements: low chill.
Other information: none available

Marglow

Synonyms: Marglo
Provenance: Unknown
Use: Dessert and culinary
Flesh colour: Yellow
Stone: Freestone
Fruit description: Large fruit with a 30% red blush on the skin.
Blossom time: Mid September—mid October
Ripening times: Late February—early March
Pollination: Self fertile
Chilling requirements: Unknown
Other information: One of the better varieties in season, but gets bacterial spot.

Marqueen

Recorded as having been grown at the Bathurst Primary Industries Centre in Australia.
Blossom time: Early September—early October
Ripening times: Mid—late February
Chilling requirements: 750 hours

Marsun

Recorded as having been grown at the Bathurst Primary Industries Centre in Australia.
Blossom time: Mid September—early October
Ripening times: Early—mid March
Chilling requirements: 850 hours

Maygold

Synonyms: May Gold
Flesh colour: Yellow
Blossom time: Mid September—mid October
Ripening times: Early—mid January

Maylady

Blossom time: Early September—late September
Ripening times: Late December—early January

MICHELINI

Synonyms: None known

Provenance: Of Unknown origin. Has been cultivated in Italy since 1930.

Use: Dessert and culinary

Flesh colour: White

Stone: Unknown

Fruit description: The fruit is round, with a red-white skin and sweet taste but does not keep well.

Blossom time: Mid September—early October

Ripening times: Mid February—early March

Pollination: Self fertile

Chilling requirements: unknown

Other information: The average tree is vigorous and large and fairly productive. Frost-tender.

Prunus persica 'Michelini'. Photo: Compagnie du Vegetal

Millicent

Provenance: Unknown
Use: Dessert and culinary
Flesh colour: White
Stone: Freestone
Fruit description: Medium sized, round, with a crimson red blush over creamy yellow background. Flesh is juicy and sweet; good flavour and texture.
Blossom time: Mid September—early October
Ripening times: Mid February
Pollination: Self fertile
Chilling requirements: Unknown
Other information: A consistent heavy bearer of good quality fruit.

Million Dollar Peach—see 'J.H. Hale'

Monroe

Recorded as having been grown at the Bathurst Primary Industries Centre in Australia.
Blossom time: Early September—early October
Ripening times: Mid February—early March
Chilling requirements: 750 hours

Newbell

A late bearing variety with juicy, delicious firm flesh. The fruit lacks the red blush that consumers prefer. Low chill.

New Flordabelle

Recorded as having been grown at the Bathurst Primary Industries Centre in Australia.
Blossom time: Early September—early October
Ripening times: Mid February—early March

O'HENRY

Synonyms: Ohenry, O Henry

Provenance: Introduced in California around 1968, O'Henry was bred by Grant Merrill and is believed to be an open pollinated seedling of Merrill Bonanza, maybe crossed with a nectarine

Use: Dessert and culinary. Lends itself to poaching and other rich peach desserts. Freezes well.

Flesh colour: Yellow (with some red streaks)

Stone: Freestone

Fruit description: Large, rounded, very firm fruit with an attractive red blush over dark yellow ground colour. Slightly fuzzy. Tough skin, rich yellow flesh. Superb flavour—very sweet, juicy and aromatic.

Blossom time: Mid September—early October

Ripening times: Mid February—early March (late ripening)

Pollination: Self fertile

Chilling requirements: 750 hours

Other information: A very popular old-fashioned peach. The O'Henry is a strong, vigorous, heavy bearing, tree, a peach leaf curl-resistant variety, tested at the WSU research station at Mt. Vernon, Washington, USA. Disease resistant and late ripening, it stores well and is an excellent shipping peach. It is extremely tasty and juicy and is similar to the yellow-skinned variety 'Million Dollar', now known as 'JH Hale'. The main difference between them is that 'JH Hale' needs a pollinator, while all other peaches and nectarines are self-fertile.

Okubo Late

Synonyms: Kubo
Provenance: The most common Pinggu peach native to Japan, where legend claims it is the original variety of peach that the Monkey King stole from the Queen Mother of the West, Guardian of the Peaches of Immortality.
Use: Dessert and culinary
Flesh colour: White
Stone: Unknown
Fruit description: A round fruit with splashes of gold against a light green background. Not as sweet as nectarines, crisp and juicy with a unique flavour.
Blossom time: Mid September—early October
Ripening times: Mid January—late January
Pollination: Self fertile
Chilling requirements: Unknown
Other information: Resistant to fungal diseases such as peach scab.

Orion

Synonyms: None known
Provenance: Unknown
Use: Dessert and culinary
Flesh colour: White
Stone: Freestone.
Fruit description: A small peach with a red blush.
Blossom time: Mid August—mid September
Ripening times: Early—mid December (early ripener)
Pollination: Self fertile
Chilling requirements: Unknown
Other information: Extremely heavy, reliable cropper; fruit often needs thinning to avoid breaking branches.

Heritage Peach Cultivars

in Australia

P to Z

Prunus Persica

Peento, Peen To, or Pan tao peaches, otherwise known as paraguayos, saturn peaches, UFO peaches, flat peaches or 'doughnut'/'donut' peaches. See: 'China Flat'

PEKIN

Recorded as having been grown at the Bathurst Primary Industries Centre in Australia.
Blossom time: Mid September—mid October
Ripening times: Early—mid January
Chilling requirements: 950 hours

PEREGRINE

Synonyms: None known
Provenance: Said to be 'the best English variety since its introduction in 1906'.
Use: Dessert and culinary
Flesh colour: White
Stone: Unknown
Fruit description: Red flushed, white skinned fruits.
Blossom time: Unknown
Ripening times: Unknown
Pollination: Self fertile
Other information: A hardy tree. Estimated time to cropping once planted: two years. Approximate time to best yields: five years.

Prunus persica 'Peregrine. Photo: Thompson & Morgan

Polar

Recorded as having been grown at the Bathurst Primary Industries Centre in Australia.
Blossom time: Mid September—early/mid October
Ripening times: Late December—mid January

Prodigiosa Morettini

Synonyms: None known
Provenance: Bred by A. Morettini in Italy, 1970 (J. H. Hale x Redhaven).
Use: Dessert and culinary
Flesh colour: Yellow
Stone: Unknown
Fruit description: Unknown
Blossom time: Mid September—early October
Ripening times: Late January—early February
Pollination: Self fertile
Chilling requirements: high chill
Other information: Matures 6-7 days before J. H. Hale, gives an excellent yield and is unusually resistant to cold. The name translates as 'Prodigious Morettini'. In the 1950s, peach breeder A. Morettini also introduced 'La Precocissima', 'La Gialla di Firenze', 'Morettini No. 1', 'Morettini No. 2', 'Prodigiosa Morettini' and 'Gialla Precoce Morettini.'

Quaresmillo

Rootstock recorded as having been grown at the Bathurst Primary Industries Centre in Australia.

Pullar

Synonyms: Pullar's Cling peach
Provenance: Unknown
Use: Dessert and culinary. Very good fruit for bottling, and fresh eating.
Flesh colour: Yellow
Stone: Clingstone
Fruit description: Large fruits, yellow flesh with red in the centre close to the stone, excellent flavour
Blossom time: Unknown
Ripening times: A very late ripener.
Pollination: Self fertile
Chilling requirements: Unknown
Other information: none

R.8.T.2.

Recorded as having been grown at the Bathurst Primary Industries Centre in Australia.
Blossom time: Early September—early October
Ripening times: Mid January—late January

Ranger

Synonyms: None known
Provenance: Unknown
Use: Dessert and culinary
Flesh colour: Red-yellow
Stone: Freestone
Fruit description: The fruit is large, and usually free of skin blemishes. Flesh is firm and will remain so for days after harvesting.
Blossom time: Early September—Early October
Ripening times: Mid—late January
Pollination: Self fertile
Chilling requirements: 900 hours.
Other information: Ranger trees are extra vigorous.

Red Cap

Syn. 'Redcap'. Recorded as having been grown at the Bathurst Primary Industries Centre in Australia.
Blossom time: Mid September—early October
Ripening times: Late December—mid January
Chilling requirements: 750 hours

Red Ceylon

Synonyms: None known
Provenance: Late in the 1880's, the 'Red Ceylon', which requires no more than 50 hours of chilling, became well-established in southern Florida, USA. In 1904, this cultivar was planted at the agricultural experiment station at Santiago de Las Vegas, Cuba, and was soon being grown all around the Havana area because it was the only peach found suitable to that tropical climate and the local soils.
Use: Dessert and culinary. Enjoy it fresh or stewed. The sliced fruit can be frozen in syrup and relished out-of-season as topping on cake or ice cream.
Flesh colour: Mainly white but a rich strawberry-red in the centre.
Stone: Freestone
Fruit description: The small fruit is oval with a protruding knob at the apex, 7 cm (2¾ in) long and 6 cm (2⅜ in) wide; velvety, green with deep-red blush when ripe. The flesh is tender, juicy, and of excellent, sweet-acid flavour having a slight suggestion of bitter-almond. The stone is free, corrugated and very hard; small in proportion to the size of the fruit.

Blossom time: Mid August—mid September
Ripening times: Unknown
Pollination: Self fertile
Chilling requirements: 50 hours (low chill).
Other information: The tree is a slender, willowy dwarf, and the small fruit has a curious little beak on its bottom. A heavy bearer. The supple branches of the 'Red Ceylon Peach' bend to the ground when laden with fruit. Despite its unattractiveness and small dimensions, the 'Red Ceylon' has delicious, finely textured flesh and is worth growing.

Red Globe

Synonyms: None known
Provenance: Not known
Use: Dessert and culinary. Complete absence of red in the flesh makes it an outstanding canning peach.
Flesh colour: Yellow
Stone: Freestone
Fruit description: A large, round fruit. Skin is highly blushed red over golden yellow background. The large size, dark red colours, and round shape make this cultivar highly attractive to the eye. Firm flesh has excellent flavour.
Blossom time: Early—late September
Ripening times: Mid—late January
Pollination: Self fertile
Chilling requirements: 850 hours
Other information: Bruise resistant fruit, a good shipper. Good quality. Trees are vigorous and productive.

Redhaven

Synonyms: Red Haven

Provenance: A hybrid of Halehaven x Kalhaven Introduced in 1940 by Dr. Stanley Johnston of Michigan (South Haven) Agricultural Experiment Station, Michigan State University, Canada, who helped revolutionise modern peach breeding.

Use: Dessert and culinary. Perfect for eating fresh, drying and stewing. Listed on 'Pick Your Own.org' Peach Varieties for Home Canning, Freezing and Preserving.

Flesh colour: Yellow

Stone: Semi-freestone

Fruit description: The fruit is round, and medium to large sized. Nearly fuzzless skin has an attractively brilliant dark red blush over a creamy yellow background. Juicy with very good flavour. The flesh has a firm, smooth texture.

Blossom time: Early September—early October

Ripening times: Mid—late January (mid season)

Pollination: Self fertile

Chilling requirements: 950 hours

Other information: Red haven was probably the most popular peach in the United States. It's the first freestone of the season and a good all-purpose peach. Vigorous, strong growing trees start to bear fruit when young. They frequently set heavy crops and must be adequately thinned to attain a good size. The crop ripens unevenly, and trees must be harvested several times. Redhaven is a superior cultivar with good winter hardiness. A popular variety for any backyard orchard. Trees grow approximately 4 x 4 metres.

Prunus persica 'Redhaven'

Red Lady

Recorded as having been grown at the Bathurst Primary Industries Centre in Australia.
Blossom time: Mid September—early October
Ripening times: Late January—early February

Red Noonan

Synonyms: None known
Provenance: Victoria, Australia, mid-20th century.
Use: Dessert and culinary. Eaten fresh or used for drying.
Flesh colour: White
Stone: Freestone
Fruit description: A delicious, rich flavour. Brilliant red skin, a very juicy medium sized, round fruit.
Blossom time: Early September—early October
Ripening times: Mid January—late January
Pollination: Self fertile
Chilling requirements: Unknown
Other information: First fruit when tree is 2 years old. A very good variety for home gardens.

Prunus persica 'Red Noonan'. Photo: Online Trees

Red Shanghai

Synonyms: Red Shangai, Red Shanghi
Provenance: A descendant of Shanghai. 'In the middle of the 19th century, some Shanghai peaches were sent to the Horticultural Society by Mr. Fortune, 'who found the tree growing to a very large size in the north of China. The flowers are very large,

the petals deeply coloured.' [Journal of the Horticultural Society as reported in Gard. Chron. 1852]. This cultivar became an important parent of hardy peach cultivars.

'Chinese Cling holds a high place in the esteem of American pomologists for its intrinsic value, because it was the first peach in one of the main stems of the peach family to arrive in America, and because it was the parent, or one of the parents, of a great number of the best white-fleshed peaches grown in that country.

'Chinese Cling created a sensation in pomology when it was brought to America because it was very different from any other peach then there, and was superior to any other in several characters. Its seedlings quickly came into prominence with the result that possibly a hundred or more of the varieties named in 'The Peaches of New York' are descended from it.'

Use: Dessert and culinary.
Flesh colour: Yellow
Stone: Semi-freestone
Fruit description: 'Fruit very large, roundish. Skin pale yellowish-green on the shaded side, and light red next the sun. Flesh pale yellow, very deep red at the stone. Melting, juicy, and richly flavoured.
Blossom time: Mid September—early October
Ripening times: Early March
Pollination: Self fertile
Chilling requirements: Unknown
Other information: 'The tree is an excellent bearer, and requires a very warm situation to ripen the fruit properly.' [Hogg – Fruit Manual p.146/1860].

Red Skin

Synonyms: Redskin
Provenance: Unknown
Use: Dessert and culinary
Flesh colour: Yellow
Stone: Freestone
Fruit description: A medium to large, good-quality peach with rich flavour. The firm flesh is covered with velvety deep red skin.
Blossom time: Early—late September
Ripening times: Early—mid February (late-ripening)
Pollination: Self fertile
Chilling requirements: 750 hours
Other information: Trees tend to be somewhat willowy but are very productive. Peaches are firm enough to ship well.

Red Queen

Synonyms: Redqueen
Recorded as having been grown at the Bathurst Primary Industries Centre in Australia.
Blossom time: Mid September—early October
Ripening times: Late January—early February

Redtop

Synonyms: Red Top
Provenance: Unknown
Use: Dessert and culinary
Flesh colour: Yellow
Stone: Freestone

Fruit description: Medium to large peach, mostly red skin with yellow background. Good flavour, sweet and slightly acid.
Blossom time: Mid September—early October
Ripening times: Mid—late January
Pollination: Self fertile

REDWING

Synonyms: Red Wing
Use: Dessert and culinary
Flesh colour: White
Stone: Unknown
Fruit description: Firm fruit, good flavour, juicy and sweet.
Blossom time: Early September—early October
Ripening times: Mid January—late January
Pollination: Self fertile

Prunus persica 'Redwing'.

REGINA

Recorded as having been grown at the Bathurst Primary Industries Centre in Australia.
Blossom time: Mid September—early October
Ripening times: Early January—mid January
Chilling requirements: 850 hours

Reids Seedling

Of Irish origin. Recorded as having been grown at the Bathurst Primary Industries Centre in Australia.
Blossom time: Mid September—mid October
Ripening times: Early—mid January

Richaven

Recorded as having been grown at the Bathurst Primary Industries Centre in Australia.
Provenance: South Haven, USA
Blossom time: Early September—early October
Ripening times: Mid—late January
Chilling requirements: 950 hours

Richlady

Synonyms: Rich Lady
Provenance: A peach released by Zaiger Genetics in California.
Use: Dessert and culinary
Flesh colour: Yellow
Stone: Semi-clingstone
Fruit description: This beautiful medium-sized peach is round and about 90% of the surface is highly coloured with dark red over a yellow-orange background. Flesh, very firm, very juicy and fine texture. The skin is moderately pubescent and the fruit is mildly aromatic. Fruit on the tree are uniform in size and shape. The flesh is dark yellow with some red pigment under the suture, and usually has less than 10% split pits. Flavour is good to excellent. Fruit is susceptible to brown rot.
Blossom time: Unknown
Ripening times: February?
Pollination: Self fertile

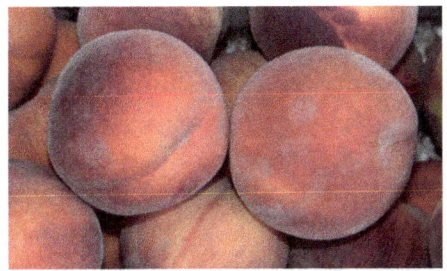

Prunus persics 'Richlady. Image: Olson Family Farms

RIO OSO GEM

Synonyms: None known.

Provenance: Rio Oso Gem was developed in the 1920's as a large, late-harvest, all-purpose peach. It is named in honor of the very small town of Rio Oso, California in the Sierra foothills.

Use: Dessert and culinary

Flesh colour: Unknown

Stone: Unknown

Fruit description: None available

Blossom time: Mid September—early October

Ripening times: Mid—late February

Pollination: Self fertile

Chilling requirements: 850 hours

Other information: Today this peach has little presence in the commercial market. The trees are small which is an advantage to a backyard grower but its overall yield is lower than that of current cultivars, and it has a tendency for fruit drop. Some say that the flesh of a Rio Oso is coarser than that of more popular peaches. The Rio Oso Gem peach is listed on the Slow Food Ark of Taste and its fruit ripens at the end of peach season.

Ron's Folly

Recorded as having been grown at the Bathurst Primary Industries Centre in Australia.
Blossom time: Mid September—early October
Ripening times: Mid—late February

Rouget

Recorded as having been grown at the Bathurst Primary Industries Centre in Australia.
Blossom time: Early September—early October
Ripening times: Unknown

Rowse Champion

Synonym 'Rouse Champion'.
Recorded as having been grown at the Bathurst Primary Industries Centre in Australia.
Blossom time: Early September—early October
Ripening times: Mid—late February

Rutgers

A rootstock grown at the Bathurst Primary Industries Centre in Australia.

Ryan Sun

Synonyms: None known
Provenance: From the USA.
Use: Dessert and culinary
Flesh colour: Yellow
Stone: Unknown
Fruit description: Large, round, firm highly coloured good quality fruit. Skin has near full red colour on a cream to yellow background. The flesh is firm, yellow and bleeding to red near the stone. Good flavour.

Blossom time: Unknown
Ripening times: Late ripening. Ripens approximately 52 days after Redhaven.
Pollination: Self fertile
Chilling requirements: Unknown

Salway

Grown by members of the Rare Fruit Society of South Australia. No other information available.

Sam Houston

Synonyms: None known
Provenance: The Sam Houston peach was developed in the 'Lone Star' state by Texas A&M.
Use: Dessert and culinary
Flesh colour: Yellow
Stone: Freestone
Fruit description: Flesh is sweet, fruit is large with a small pit.
Blossom time: Early September—late September
Ripening times: Mid—late January
Pollination: Self fertile
Chilling requirements: 500 chill hours

Prunus persica 'Sam Houston'. Photo: Willis Orchard Co.

San Pedro

Synonyms: None known
Provenance: San Pedro originated in the USA and was released in South Africa in 1985.
Use: Dessert and culinary
Flesh colour: Yellow
Stone: Clingstone
Fruit description: The flesh is light yellow. The taste is good, slightly acid and the texture is melting and fine. The colourful red skin has a bright yellow ground colour. The shape is slightly oblong.
Blossom time: Mid August—mid September
Ripening times: Late December
Pollination: Self fertile
Chilling requirements: Unknown

Sentinel

Synonyms: None known
Provenance: One of the peach varieties that 'Texas A & M University Agrilife Extension' recommends for growing in the warmer climes of Texas.
Use: Dessert and culinary
Flesh colour: Unknown
Stone: Semi-freestone
Fruit description: A large, round, red-blushed peach. Good flavour and texture.
Blossom time: Early September—early October
Ripening times: Early—mid January
Pollination: Self fertile
Chilling requirements: 850 hours
Other information: A strong, vigorous and productive tree. Survives hot, cold and freezing temperatures.

Prunus persica 'Sentinel'

SHERMAN'S EARLY

Recorded as having been grown at the Bathurst Primary Industries Centre in Australia.
Blossom time: Late August—mid/late September
Ripening times: Late November—mid December

SHERMAN'S RED

Recorded as having been grown at the Bathurst Primary Industries Centre in Australia.
Blossom time: Late August—late September
Ripening times: Mid—late December

Shippers Late Red

Synonyms: Shippers Late
Provenance: Unknown
Use: Dessert and culinary
Flesh colour: Unknown
Stone: Unknown
Fruit description: Rich, red colouring on the skin. Excellent flavour.
Blossom time: Mid September—early October
Ripening times: Early—mid February
Pollination: Self fertile
Chilling requirements: 850 hours
Other information: In the *Gettysburg Times* (USA) on September 6, 1946, H.J. Oyler's Packing House advertised Shippers Late Red peaches for sale.
In 1958 the leading variety in Blount County, TN., USA, was Shippers Late Red, with about 11,000 trees in production.

Siberian C

A rootstock grown at the Bathurst Primary Industries Centre in Australia.

Somervee

Synonyms: None known
Provenance: Named and introduced in 1950. Bred at Ontario Station (Canada) from a cross between Halehaven and Oriole.
Use: Dessert and culinary
Flesh colour: Yellow
Stone: Clingstone

Fruit description: The fruit is medium sized, round, well coloured, attractive. and of good quality for so early a variety.
Blossom time: Mid—early September
Ripening times: Late December—early January (early ripener)
Pollination: Self fertile
Chilling requirements: Unknown
Other information: Trees bear well. Fruit requires thinning.

Southland

Synonyms: None known
Provenance: The Southland peach, introduced in 1946, is seedling of 'selfed' (self-fertilised) Halehaven.
Use: Dessert and culinary
Flesh colour: Yellow
Stone: Freestone
Fruit description: The fruit is medium-sized to large and round and has light pubescence. About half the surface is covered with a red blush, lighter than the blush of the parent, Halehaven. The ground colour is attractive yellow. The flesh is firm, slow-softening, juicy, medium-textured, melting, ripening evenly except for slight tendency to ripen at base first, and with a delicious, mild flavour.
Blossom time: Early September—early October
Ripening times: Mid—late January
Pollination: Self fertile
Chilling requirements: 750 hours
Other information: The tree is vigorous, productive, upright to slightly spreading. The fruit is slow to soften after picking, which means it ships well.

SPRINGCREST

Synonyms: Spring Crest
Provenance: Unknown
Use: Dessert and culinary
Flesh colour: Yellow
Stone: Freestone
Fruit description: Large fruit with beautiful colour and very little fuzz. Best eaten after ripening on the tree.
Blossom time: Early September—early October
Ripening times: Mid—late December
Pollination: Self fertile
Chilling requirements: 650 hours

Prunus persica 'Springcrest'

Prunus persica 'Springold'

SPRINGOLD

Synonyms: Spring Gold
Provenance: Unknown
Use: Dessert and culinary
Flesh colour: Yellow
Stone: Freestone
Fruit description: Good fruit size
Blossom time: Early September—early October
Ripening times: Early—mid December (early ripener)
Pollination: Self fertile
Chilling requirements: 850 hours

Stark Early Glo

Synonyms: Stark's Early Glow, Early Glow

Provenance: In 1816, American James Hart Stark moved by horse-drawn wagon from Kentucky to Louisiana, Missouri. He took with him a bundle of apple scions. From his bundle he started a nursery business. Stark Brothers Nurseries have been growing and breeding fruit trees since 1815. They collaborated with renowned horticulturist Luther Burbank, who willed over 750 of his varieties to the company. This peach is one of Stark's older cultivars that has passed into the public domain.

Use: Dessert and culinary
Flesh colour: Unknown
Stone: Unknown
Fruit description: none available
Blossom time: Early September—early October
Ripening times: Late December—early January
Pollination: Self fertile
Chilling requirements: Unknown

Starking Delicious

Synonyms: None known.

Provenance: In the 1960s Stark Nurseries set out to develop a version of the July Elberta that could be harvested earlier. Starking Delicious was the result.

Use: Dessert and culinary. These peaches have firm skin that slips off easily, making them perfect for canning and freezing.

Flesh colour: Yellow
Stone: Freestone

Prunus persica 'Starking Delicious'. Photo: Stark Bros.

Fruit description: Medium to large sized peaches are coloured a rich red. The flesh is of a medium-firm texture, juicy and moderately sweet.
Blossom time: Early September—early October
Ripening times: Early—mid January
Pollination: Self fertile
Chilling requirements: not known
Other information: a strong, vigorous tree that takes two to four years to bear, and produces fruit three weeks earlier than July Elberta and 5-6 weeks earlier than Elberta. Note: there are also an apple and a pear by the same name.

Stowell

Recorded as having been grown at the Bathurst Primary Industries Centre in Australia.
Blossom time: Early/mid September—mid October
Ripening times: Early April

Summer Glo

Synonyms: Summer Glow
Provenance: Unknown
Use: Dessert and culinary
Flesh colour: Yellow
Stone: Freestone
Fruit description: Round shape, with a dark red skin and very good flavour. A fine crisp texture and firm, melting flesh.
Blossom time: Early September—early October
Ripening times: Mid—late January
Pollination: Self fertile
Chilling requirements: Medium
Other information: Stores well. A vigorous tree and fairly productive.

Summerset

Synonyms: None known
Provenance: Unknown
Use: Dessert and culinary. Excellent for canning, freezing or fresh eating.
Flesh colour: Yellow
Stone: Freestone
Fruit description: Large, sweet and flavourful.
Blossom time: Early September—early October
Ripening times: Late February—early March
Pollination: Self fertile
Chilling requirements: 700 hours below 7°C (45°F)

Suncrest

Synonyms: Sun Crest
Provenance: Originated in Fresno, CA. Introduced in 1959.
Use: Dessert and culinary
Flesh colour: Yellow
Stone: Freestone
Fruit description: Large, round, attractive peach. About 80% bright red blush over yellow background. Flesh is exceptionally firm with good texture and flavour. Fragrant and juicy.
Blossom time: Not known
Ripening times: Not known
Pollination: Self fertile
Chilling requirements: 500 hours.
Other information: Vigorous, heavy-bearing trees. One source declares that the fruit ships very well. Ark of Taste, on the other hand, says 'Unfortunately, not much is known of the Sun Crest. Because of its fragility and difficulty in shipping, distributors and retailers are unwilling to handle the fruit.'

Sunhaven

Synonyms: Sun Haven
Provenance: South Haven, USA
Use: Dessert and culinary. Flesh resists browning so this peach is ideal for canning and bottling.
Flesh colour: Yellow
Stone: Freestone

Fruit description: Richly flavoured peaches, bright red with yellow-gold cheeks. Tender flesh that resists browning.
Blossom time: Early September—early October
Ripening times: Early—mid January
Pollination: Self fertile
Chilling requirements: Unknown
Other information: Vigorous, productive, hardy to —19°.

Prunus persica 'Sunhaven. Photo: Miller Nurseries

Sunhigh

Synonyms: Sun High
Provenance: not known
Use: Dessert and culinary. Excellent for eating, freezing, and canning.
Flesh colour: Yellow
Stone: Freestone
Fruit description: A large oval-shaped easy to pick peach, with a sweet flavour similar to the Loring.
Blossom time: Mid September—early October
Ripening times: Late January—early February
Pollination: Self fertile
Chilling requirements: 750 hours

SUNNYSIDE

Synonyms: Sunny Side
Provenance: United States Department of Agriculture, Fresno, California, 1974
Use: Dessert and culinary
Flesh colour: Unknown
Stone: Freestone
Fruit description: Unknown
Blossom time: Late Aug—late September
Ripening times: Early—mid January
Pollination: Self fertile
Chilling requirements: low chill

SUNQUEEN

Synonyms: Sun Queen
Provenance: 'Sunqueen' was introduced in the autumn of 1966 by the New Jersey Agricultural Experiment Station.
Use: Dessert and culinary
Flesh colour: Unknown
Stone: Unknown
Fruit description: Unknown
Blossom time: Early September—early October
Ripening times: Unknown
Pollination: Self fertile
Chilling requirements: Unknown

SUNRAY

Synonyms: Sun Ray
Provenance: South Africa. Released 1964.
Use: Dessert and culinary
Flesh colour: Yellow
Stone: Clingstone
Fruit description: The shape is round with a point. The skin is covered with over 70% red blush. Fruit is firm and the light yellow flesh has a melting texture. Good eating quality.
Blossom time: Early—late September
Ripening times: Mid—late December
Pollination: Self fertile
Chilling requirements: medium (401 - 600 Infruitec chilling units).
Other information: The tree is not very vigorous, however it produces a reasonable crop each year and the fruit stores moderately well—i.e. for up to three weeks.

Prunus persica 'Sunray'. Photo: Agricultural Research Council

Suwanee

Synonyms: None known.

Provenance: Named for Suwanee, a city in Gwinnett County in the U.S. state of Georgia.

Use: Dessert and culinary

Flesh colour: Yellow

Stone: Freestone

Fruit description: A beautiful large medium-soft peach that bears heavily in low-chill winter areas and coastal areas. Suwanee peach has a deliciously sweet, mild flavour.

Blossom time: Early—late September

Ripening times: Mid—late January

Pollination: Self fertile

Chilling requirements: 500 chill hours

Prunus persica 'Suwanee'. Photo: Willis Orchards.

Sweet Nipple

This cultivar is recorded as held by the Rare Fruit Society of South Australia. No other information is available.

Tatura 204

Synonyms: T204

Provenance: An Australian-bred peach, one of a series of clingstones developed in the 1980s at the town of Tatura in the peach-growing Goulburn Valley region of Victoria, Australia.

Use: Dessert and culinary. Excellent for bottling because retains shape well (and sweet enough to bottle with little or no sugar).

Flesh colour: Yellow

Stone: Clingstone

Fruit description: Medium to large, golden yellow skin with firm, juicy, sweet, non-melting flesh.

Blossom time: Unknown

Ripening times: Unknown

Pollination: Self fertile

Chilling requirements: Unknown

Prunus persica 'Tatura 204'. Photo: NZ Fruit Tree Company

Tatura 211

Synonyms: T211:

Provenance: An Australian-bred peach, one of a series of clingstones developed in the 1980s at the town of Tatura in the peach-growing Goulburn Valley region of Victoria, Australia.

Use: Dessert and culinary, escpecially canning and bottling.

Flesh colour: Yellow

Stone: Clingstone

Fruit description: Very similar to T204 but slightly darker skin. Very large, average fruit size 80mm. Skin has an orange-red blush on a yellow background. Firm flesh, good flavour, sweet and juicy.

Blossom time: Unknown

Ripening times: Mid February, overlaps with the last week's harvest of Tatura 204

Pollination: Self fertile

Chilling requirements: Unknown

Other information: More prolific bearer than T204.

Tatura Aurora

This cultivar is recorded as held by the Rare Fruit Society of South Australia. No other information is available.

Taylor Queen

Use: Dessert and culinary. Along with 'Golden Queen', 'Taylor Queen' is one of the canning peaches in the Goulburn Valley region of Australia. Excellent for bottling, too.

Flesh colour: Yellow

Stone: Clingstone
Fruit description: Very similar to Golden Queen, but tends to be slightly smaller fruit. Very sweet.
Pollination: Self fertile

Trethowan No.1.

Recorded as having been grown at the Bathurst Primary Industries Centre in Australia.
Blossom time: Mid September—early October. No other information available.

Trethowan No.2.

Recorded as having been grown at the Bathurst Primary Industries Centre in Australia.
Blossom time: Mid September—early October. No other information available.

Triogem

Synonyms: None known
Provenance: USA
Use: Dessert and culinary. An outstanding peach for freezing.
Flesh colour: Unknown
Stone: Freestone
Fruit description: Medium-large, very attractive fruit, bright red over whole surface.
Blossom time: Mid September—early October
Ripening times: Mid—late January
Pollination: Self fertile
Chilling requirements: Unknown
Other information: Very productive

Tropic Beauty

Synonyms: TropicBeauty

Provenance: USA

Use: Dessert and culinary

Flesh colour: Yellow

Stone: Semi-freestone,

Fruit description: Medium-sized, red-skinned peach. Soft, melting, flesh with excellent flavour. Very attractive in colour, excellent shape and very firm, but very susceptible to bacterial spot.

Blossom time: Unknown

Ripening times: mid season

Pollination: Self fertile

Chilling requirements: 150 chill hours.

Prunus persica 'Tropic Beauty. Photo: Just Fruits and Exotics

Tropic Snow

Synonyms: TropicSnow

Provenance: USA

Use: Dessert and culinary. Non-browning flesh makes it a good canning or bottling peach.

Flesh colour: White

Stone: Freestone

Fruit description: A round, firm peach, medium to large, with creamy white skin with light red overcolour, sweet, low acid flesh and outstanding flavour.

Blossom time: Unknown

Ripening times: Unknown

Pollination: Self fertile

Chilling requirements: 200 - 225 hours

Other information: Highly resistant to bacterial spot.

Prunus persica 'Tropic Snow'. Photo: Just Fruits and Exotics

Troy

Synonyms: None known
Provenance: Troy resulted from a cross of Raritan Rose (a white fleshed freestone) x Redskin (a yellow fleshed freestone). It was released in 1968.
Use: Dessert and culinary
Flesh colour: Unknown
Stone: Freestone
Fruit description: Unknown
Blossom time: Mid September—early October
Ripening times: Mid—late January
Pollination: Self fertile
Chilling requirements: 950 hours
Other information: Troy has had an inconsistent cropping record, producing light crops in some years. In many years, only very light or no fruit thinning will be required. Very few split pits have been observed. Trees are vigorous.

Tulip

Recorded as having been grown at the Bathurst Primary Industries Centre in Australia.
Blossom time: Mid September—mid October
Ripening times: Late December—mid January

Tyler

Synonyms: None known
Provenance: Unknown
Use: Dessert and culinary
Flesh colour: Unknown
Stone: Unknown
Fruit description: Flesh has a medium-firm texture

Blossom time: Mid September—early October
Ripening times: Early February—mid February
Pollination: Self fertile
Chilling requirements: 950 hours

Velvet

Recorded as having been grown at the Bathurst Primary Industries Centre in Australia.
Blossom time: Early/mid September—early October
Ripening times: Mid—late January
Chilling requirements: 950 hours

Vesper

Synonyms: None known
Provenance: From Ontario Station, Canada. Named and introduced in 1949. Vesper is a cross of J. H. Hale and Vedette, and was sent out for grower trial in 1939.
Use: Dessert and culinary
Flesh colour: Yellow
Stone: Freestone
Fruit description: The fruit is well-coloured, attractive, medium to large size, good quality, nice flavour.
Blossom time: Early September—early October
Ripening times: Mid—late February
Pollination: Self fertile
Chilling requirements: Unknown
Other information: The tree has fair vigour only, and is susceptible to bacterial leaf spot in some seasons. It bears regularly.

W. H. Spinks

This peach cultivar is recorded as having been grown at the Bathurst Primary Industries Centre in Australia.

The only material possibly linked to this fruit is as follows, from *The Sydney Morning Herald*, Thursday 5 July 1934:

'An extremely wide range of subjects is being discussed by a conference of fruit instructors and orchardists now being held under the guidance of the director of fruit culture (Mr. C G Savage), at Hawkesbury Agricultural College. The subjects set down for discussion on the first day relate chiefly to insect and fungus pests. The root nematode is being dealt with by Mr W. H. Spinks.'

Walgant

Synonyms: None known
Provenance: South Africa. Released 1959
Use: Dessert and culinary. Good canning quality.
Flesh colour: Yellow
Stone: Clingstone
Fruit description: The fruit is ovate in shape, the flesh deep yellow-orange, with a very firm, non-melting texture. Diameter of fruit is usually around 60mm, mass 140g. Good eating quality.
Blossom time: Not known
Ripening times: Not known
Pollination: Self fertile
Chilling requirements: medium (401 - 600 Infruitec chilling units).
Other information: a vigorous tree. The peaches store well.

Prunus persica 'Walgant'. Photo: Agricultural Research Council

WATT'S EARLY

Recorded as having been grown at the Bathurst Primary Industries Centre in Australia. Possibly a synonym for 'Watt's Early Champion', a cultivar that was popular in Australia in the 1940s and 1950s.

WHITE ELBERTA

This cultivar is recorded as held by the Rare Fruit Society of South Australia. No other information is available.

Whynot

Synonyms: None known

Provenance: Whynot is an open-pollinated seedling of Erly-Red-Fre. It was released in 1968.

Use: Dessert and culinary, but best eaten fresh.

Flesh colour: Yellow

Stone: Clingstone

Fruit description: Fruit are round and attractive with short pubescence and a slightly pronounced suture and tip. The skin is 75% bright red with a medium yellow ground colour. The flesh is firm, melting, slightly coarse and has good flavour for an early-ripening peach. Flesh colour is medium yellow with very little red at the pit cavity.

Blossom time: Not known

Ripening times: one of the earliest ripening cultivars available.

Pollination: Self fertile

Chilling requirements: 950 hours

Other information: Fruit production from Whynot is only fair to good, with light crops in some years. This is due in part to the tendency of Whynot to produce a low number of flower buds in many years. Thus, little or no fruit thinning is necessary. Because Whynot fruit ripen so early, fruit size is small 4 to 5cm (1.5 to 2 inches) and thinning, if necessary, must be carried out early to obtain maximum fruit size. The flesh browns very rapidly when exposed to air. Whynot trees are of medium vigour and resistant to bacterial spot.

WIGGINS

Synonyms: None known

Provenance: A classic, old-fashioned heritage peach.

Use: Dessert and culinary. Great for eating fresh or bottling.

Flesh colour: White

Stone: Unknown

Fruit description: Juicy and very sweet, good quality, doesn't have the colour of some modern varieties, but the flavour is superb.

Blossom time: Unknown

Ripening times: Unknown

Pollination: Self fertile

Chilling requirements: Unknown

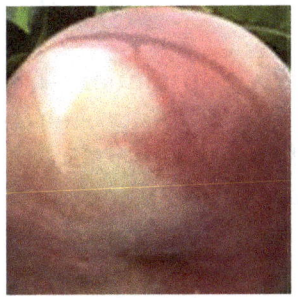

Prunus persica 'Wiggins'

WILLOWLEAF ELBERTA

This cultivar is recorded as held by the Rare Fruit Society of South Australia. No other information is available.

Winblo

Synonyms: Windblo

Provenance: Winblo resulted from an open-pollinated seedling of Redskin. It was released in 1972.

Use: Dessert and culinary. The flesh is very resistant to flesh browning, which makes this a good peach for canning and bottling.

Flesh colour: Yellow

Stone: Freestone

Fruit description: Fruits are round with extremely short and sparse pubescence. The skin colour is very attractive, with 75% of the fruit surface a bright red blush over a light yellow ground colour. Fruit of Winblo are large. The flesh has average firmness, fine texture and is light yellow in colour. Flavour is excellent. The pit is free from the flesh at maturity and the fruit are very resistant to split-pitting.

Blossom time: Early September—early October

Ripening times: Late January—early February

Pollination: Self fertile

Chilling requirements: 800 hours

Other information: It has a good to excellent crop production history and will require fruit thinning in most years. Trees of Winblo are vigorous and moderately resistant to bacterial spot.

Wotton Early

Recorded as having been grown at the Bathurst Primary Industries Centre in Australia.

Blossom time: Early September—early October

Ripening times: Early—mid January

Wrights Cling

This cultivar is recorded as held by the Rare Fruit Society of South Australia. No other information is available.

Wrights Early

This cultivar is recorded as held by the Rare Fruit Society of South Australia. No other information is available.

Xmas Box

Recorded as having been grown at the Bathurst Primary Industries Centre in Australia. Judging by the name, it ripens around 25th December. No other information is available.

Yakima Hale

Synonyms: None known.
Provenance: The Yakima Hale is one of the older, more historic American peach varieties dating back to its selection in 1955 in Red Bluff, California, by Mr. J.H. Hale.
Use: Dessert and culinary
Flesh colour: Yellow
Stone: Freestone
Fruit description: Large fruit, skin is pale yellow with some orange colouring.
Blossom time: Early September—early October
Ripening times: Unknown
Pollination: Self fertile
Chilling requirements: Unknown

Zeelady

Synonyms: None known

Provenance: Developed by Zaiger's Genetics. U.S. Plant Patent No. 5832 (expired). Zaiger's Genetics. located in Modesto, California USA, is a company that breeds fruit trees. They run the largest stone fruit breeding programme in the world. This second generation family business was established during the 1960's. Floyd Zaiger (born 1926) is a biologist who is most noted for his work in fruit genetics, and founded the company. He uses cross-pollination, rather than gene-splicing or DNA manipulation, to develop new hybrids. Zaiger's Genetics have created fruits such as the Aprium (apricot and plum), the Nectarcot (nectarine and apricot), Peacotum (peach, apricot and plum) and the pluot (plum and apricot).

Use: Dessert and culinary. Good for freezing.

Flesh colour: Yellow

Stone: Freestone

Fruit description: Bright red, very large, delicious balanced flavour. Lovely skin colour; 80% to 90% bright red over yellow.

Blossom time: Unknown

Ripening times: Midseason

Pollination: Self fertile

Chilling requirements: 900-1,000 hours

Other information: The tree is a heavy producer.

Prunus persica 'Zee Lady'. Photo: Dave Wilson Nursery

ENDNOTE:

In the mid 1920s Italian horticulturists, both amateur and professional, developed well-organised large-scale peach breeding programmes with the aim of creating improved cultivars. Among these pioneers was a scientist named A. Morettini, who worked at the University of Florence. His work, which continued for 30 years, concentrated on crossing American yellow-fleshed peach varieties with nectarines. In particular he used the cultivar J.H. Hale, which was held to be the best peach of its era.

Eventually he bred approximately twenty cultivars of both yellow and white fleshed peaches. These new fruits ripened over a period of almost three months, greatly extending the harvest season.

ACKNOWLEDGMENTS

Agricultural Research Council, 1134 Park Street, Hatfield, Pretoria, South Africa

Balhanna Nurseries, Hartmann Rd., Charleston South Australia 5244

bib.ge image website, Georgia, Soviet Union

Bylands Nurseries, 1600 Byland Rd, Kelowna, British Columbia, Canada

Chestnut Hill Tree Farm, Florida, USA

Compagnie du Vegetal, Saint-Etienne, France

Dave Wilson Wholesale Nursery, California USA

Edible Gardens, Palmerston North, New Zealand

Florida Gardener website: www.floridagardener.com

Garden Express 470 Monbulk Rd., Monbulk VIC 3793 Australia

Hawkes Bay Clean, Stone Fruit Growers, New Zealand.

Homeguides, San Francisco Chronicle, 901 Mission St, San Francisco, California USA

Just Fruits and Exotics, North Florida, USA

Milan Havlis Garden Centre, Prague, Czech Republic

Miller Nurseries, 5060 County Road 16, Canandaigua, New York State, USA

Mount Alexander Fruit Gardens, 69 Danns Rd, Harcourt VIC 3453 Australia

NZ Fruit Tree Company, P.O. Box 446 Hastings, New Zealand

Olea Nurseries, RMB 44 Mitchelldean Road, Manjimup, Western Australia 6258

Pete's Produce Farm, 1225 East Street Road, West Chester, Pennsylvania 19382 USA

Thompson & Morgan, Poplar Lane, Ipswich, Suffolk, UK

Index

A

Abiacuto 3
Afterglow 3
Albatros 3
Anzac 3

B

Baby Gold 5 4
Baby Gold 6 4
Beale 5
Bendigo Beauty 5
Blackburn 5
Blackburn Elberta 6
Blackman 6
Blake 6
Boon County Seedling 6
Boyce-Elberta 7
Briggs Red May 7
Brighton 8

C

Candoka 8
Candor 11
Cardinal 13
Carman 13
Champion 14
China Flat 14
Clayton 15
Collins 16
Colonel 16
Comanche 16
Cornish 17
Corona 17
Coronet 17
Corowa 18
Correll 18
Cresthaven xxxiii, 19, 63
Curraearly 19

D

Desertgold 20
Desert Red 21
De Wet 20
Dixigem 22
Dixired 23
Doncaster Crawford 24
Dripstone Elberta 24
Dwarf Valley Red 24

E

Earlibelle 29
Earligrande 30
Earlired 31
Early O'Henry 31
Elberta xxxiii, 5, 6, 7, 24, 26, 31, 32, 33, 39, 62, 63, 71, 72, 73, 75, 111, 112, 127, 129
Ellerbe 33
Emery 34
Erly-Red-Fre 35

F

Fairhaven 36, 63
Fairtime 37
Fairway 38
Favorita I 38
Favorita II 38
Fay 3 38
Fay 4 39
Fay Elberta 39
Fayette 40
Fertila Morettini 41
Fire Prince 41
Flamecrest 42
Flavorcrest 43
Flordabeauty 43
Flordabelle 44
Flordacrest 45
Flordagem 46
Flordaglo 46
Flordagold 47
Flordagrande 48
Flordahome 49
Flordaking 49
Flordaprince 50
Flordaqueen 51
Flordared 52
Flordastar 53
Flordasun 53
Florida xxi, 26, 27, 28, 43, 44, 45, 46, 47, 48, 49, 50, 51, 52, 53, 83, 94
Florida Peaches 26
Fragar xxxiii, 54
Frome 54

G

Galston Red 54
Garnet Beauty 55
Glenalton 56
Glohaven 56, 63
Golden Amber 57
Golden Gem 57
Golden Queen xxv, xxxiii, 57, 120, 121
Golden Red 57
Greys 58
Guame Cling 58

H

Halehaven 23, 33, 62, 64, 75, 96, 108, 109
Harbelle 65
Harbinger 65
Harbrite 66
Harken 67
Harmony 68
Harrow xxi, 55, 60, 61, 66, 69
Harrow Peaches 60
Haruko 68
Haven xxi, 19, 22, 36, 56, 62, 64, 75, 96, 102, 114
Haven Peaches 62
Havis 69
Hiland 69
Honey Dew Hale 70

I

Idlewild 70
Inquee 70
Ireland's Peach 70

J

Jersey Queen 72
J H Hale 71, 72
J H Hale Hitchcock 72
Julie 72
July Elberta 72
June Lady 74
June Prince 75

K

Kalhaven 62, 75, 96
Keystone 76
Kingston 76
Kirkman 76
Klamt 76

L

La Feliciana 78
La Gem 79
La Gold 79
La Premier 79
La Red 79
Late Hale 79
Late Italian Red 80
Late Loring 81
Late Loring Thomas 81
Le Vainquer 81
Loring xxxiii, 81, 82, 115

M

Madison 82
Maravilha 83
Marglow 83
Marqueen 84
Marsun 84
Maygold 84
Maylady 84
Michelini 85
Millicent 86
Million Dollar Peach - see 'J.H. Hale' 86
Monroe 86
Morettini 38, 41, 92, 134

N

Newbell 86
New Flordabelle 86

O

O'Henry xxxiii, 31, 87
Okubo Late 88
Orion 88

P

Peento 14, 90
Pekin 91
Peregrine 91
Polar 92
Prodigiosa Morettini 92
Pullar 93

Q

Quaresmillo 92

R

R.8.T.2. 93
Ranger 93
Red Cap 94
Red Ceylon 94
Red Globe 95

Redhaven xxxiii, 11, 12, 26, 33,
    55, 62, 63, 92, 96, 97, 105
Red Lady 97
Red Noonan 98
Red Queen 100
Red Shanghai 98
Red Skin 100
Redtop 100
Redwing 101
Regina 101
Reids Seedling 102
Richaven 63, 102
Richlady 102
Rio Oso Gem 103
Ron's Folly 104
Rouget 104
Rowse Champion 104
Rutgers 104
Ryan Sun 104

S

Salway 105
Sam Houston 105
San Pedro 106
Sentinel 106
Sherman's Early 107
Sherman's Red 107
Shippers Late Red 108
Siberian C 108
Somervee 108
Southland 109
Springcrest 110
Springold 110
Stark Early Glo 111
Starking Delicious 111
Stowell 113

Summerset 113
Suncrest 114
Sunhaven 63, 65, 114, 115
Sunhigh 115
Sunnyside 116
Sunqueen 116
Sunray 117
Suwanee 118
Sweet Nipple 119

T

Tatura 204 119
Tatura 211 120
Tatura Aurora 120
Taylor Queen 120
Trethowan No.1. 121
Trethowan No.2. 121
Triogem 121
Tropic Beauty 122
Tropic Snow 123
Troy 124
Tulip 124
Tyler 124

V

Velvet 125
Vesper 125

W

Walgant 126
Watt's Early 127
White Elberta 127
W.H.Spinks 126
Whynot 128
Wiggins 129

Willowleaf Elberta 129
Winblo 130
Wotton Early 130
Wrights Cling 131
Wrights Early 131

X

Xmas Box 131

Y

Yakima Hale 131

Z

Zeelady xxxiii, 132

Some Heritage Fruit Groups in Australia

Werribee Park Heritage Orchard, situated near Melbourne, Victoria (Australia) is a beautiful antique orchard dating from the 1870s, on the grounds of the old mansion by the Werribee River. It was renowned for its peaches, grapes, apples, quinces, pears, a variety of plums and several other fruits, as well as walnuts and olives. Over the past few decades the orchard was forgotten and—through neglect—fell into ruin. Recently this historic treasure has been rediscovered. Volunteers are replanting and tending the orchard.

The Heritage Fruits Society is based in Melbourne, Australia. Their aim is to conserve heritage fruit varieties on private and public land. They enable and encourage society members to research this wide range of varieties and to inform the public on the benefits of heritage fruits for health, sustainability and biodiversity.

Petty's Orchard in Templestowe, Victoria, Australia, is one of Melbourne's oldest commercial orchards, and it holds the largest collection of heritage/heirloom apple varieties on mainland Australia, with more than two hundred varieties of old and rare apples. The maintenance of the apple tree collection is done by Heritage Fruits Society volunteers.

The Rare Fruit Society of South Australia is an amateur organisation of fruit tree growers who preserve heritage varieties, explore climate limitations and study propagation, pruning and grafting techniques.

www.ingramcontent.com/pod-product-compliance
Lightning Source LLC
Chambersburg PA
CBHW050636160426
43194CB00010B/1695